ROCK WIVES

THE HARD LIVES
AND GOOD TIMES
OF THE WIVES,
GIRLFRIENDS,
AND GROUPIES
OF ROCK AND ROLL

Victoria Balfour

Photographs by Harvey Wang

BTB
BEECH TREE BOOKS
WILLIAM MORROW
New York

Library of Congress Cataloging-in-Publication Data

Balfour, Victoria.
  Rock wives.

    1. Rock musicians' wives—Biography. 2. Groupies—
Biography. 3. Rock musicians—Biography. I. Wang,
Harvey. II. Title.
ML394.B34 1986   784.5′4′00922 [B]   85-13525
ISBN 0-688-04386-0

Printed in the United States of America

First Edition

1 2 3 4 5 6 7 8 9 10

BOOK DESIGN BY RICHARD ORIOLO

The word "book" is said to derive from *boka*, or beech.
The beech tree has been the patron tree of writers since ancient times and
represents the flowering of literature and knowledge.

For my parents

ACKNOWLEDGMENTS

To all the people who consented to be interviewed for this book, whether they appear in these pages or not, many, many thanks.

Sincere thanks also to: Laura Adler, Francesca Belanger, Rob Brill, Harold Bronson, Marcelle Clements, Irwin Cohen, Nick Cowan, David Dalton, Liz Derringer, Stan Diamond, Randy Dunlap, Jane Friedman, Kate Gaffin, Hadassah Gold, Suzy Greene, Jennie Halsall, Gerri Hirshey, Bianca Jagger, Bob Love, Gregory May, Mary McCarthy, John Milward, Terry Moore, Michael Ochs, Curt Pesmen, Jim Pewter, Carla Rotolo, Connie Schrait, Fred Schrucrs, Howard Siegal, David Walley, Ian Whitcomb, Jamie Wolff, Bobby Wolliver, Robert Zappa.

The following books and magazines have been very useful in my research: David Dalton's *The Rolling Stones—The First Twenty Years*; Philip Norman's *Symphony for the Devil*; Anthony Scaduto's *Bob Dylan*; Jerry Hopkins and Danny Sugerman's *No One Here Gets Out Alive*; Charles White's *The Life and Times of Little Richard*; Myra Lewis's *Great Balls of Fire*; Angie Bowie's *Free Spirit*; *The Rolling Stone Encyclopedia of Rock and Roll*; Brock Helander's *The Rock Who's Who*; *Rolling Stone*; *People*; *The New York Times*; the New York *Daily News*; the New York *Post*.

I must thank especially my agent, Carol Mann, for her support. Also Harvey Wang, the photographer, for all of his help, energy, and enthusiasm. Many thanks to James Landis for all his editorial guidance.

Finally, deepest thanks to Jim Fitzgerald for his inspiration, encouragement, patience, and humor. Without him this book could not have been written.

CONTENTS

INTRODUCTION

Ever since rock and roll shocked the world and revolutionized the music scene in the mid-fifties, female fans have related to its stars as sexual objects. Whether it was Elvis, the Beatles, or Duran Duran, women have worked themselves into a frenzy over rock and roll singers, screaming, fainting, and weeping at rock concerts or stampeding the stage in the hopes of getting just one touch of their idols. I was no exception. When I got my first glimpse of the Beatles on *The Ed Sullivan Show* in 1964 at age nine, I was hooked. The Beatles had unleashed some sexual feelings in me, and from that night on, I became an obsessive Beatlemaniac. I mooned and sighed over their pictures and I screamed as loud as anyone throughout their twenty-five-minute-long concert at Toronto's Maple Leaf Gardens on Labor Day in '64. I bought up Beatle bubble gum cards, Beatle posters, Beatle wigs, Beatle 45s, and Beatle rugs (I wanted to decorate my bedroom with Beatle wallpaper, but my mother drew the line on that one).

Of course, like every true-blue female Beatlemaniac, I had a favorite, Paul. I considered myself lucky that I had chosen him—I remember how upset some of my friends were who liked John Lennon when the words "Sorry, girls, he's married" appeared on the screen under his name during the *Sullivan Show*. At any rate, I liked to make up fantasies about how Paul and I would meet and how he would fall for an older, more sophisticated me. I *had* to know every personal detail about him, so I devoured the teen fan magazines. From *16 Magazine* and *Tiger Beat* I learned that Paul's favorite food was steak and chips, his favorite clothes black polo-necked sweaters, and—most important—his girl-friend was a red-headed actress named Jane Asher. I soon became as obsessed about finding out all there was to know about Jane as I had been with Paul. It seems other fans were too, for as time went on, the fan magazines stepped up their coverage of Jane and the other Beatle girlfriends and wives, not to mention the Rolling Stones' ladies. It got to the point where some of the rock girlfriends became so popular that they had their own columns in the magazines. Beatle George Harrison's girlfriend (and later wife), Patti Boyd, dispensed such tips as how to make your bangs look like hers (cut them shorter in the middle, longer at the sides) in her own beauty column for *16 Magazine*. Mick Jagger's then-girlfriend Chrissie Shrimpton reported on the swinging London music and social scene in *her* column, "From London with Luv" for *Mod* magazine. A typical entry went something along these lines: "I think Stevie Winwood with the Spencer Davis Group is a fantastic singer. In fact the best singer we have (ouch! Mick just hit me!)."

By the late sixties, rock and roll was well on its way to becoming a huge money-making business, and the establishment had begun to embrace the rock stars wholeheartedly. Gossip columnists at major dailies began to report regularly on the goings-on of the rock stars; *Life* magazine did cover stories on them. Accordingly, the rock wives and girlfriends became more acceptable, too. Suddenly, I began to see women like Patti Boyd in the pages of my mother's issues of *Vogue* and *Harper's Bazaar*. And by the time the seventies rolled around, the rock women had definitely become major celebrities simply by virtue of their men's celebrity. For instance, nobody had heard of Bianca Perez Mora Macias before she married Mick Jagger in 1971, but after her marriage she was deluged with movie and modeling offers and was praised by fashion experts for her "style."

Public reaction to the rock wives was not always favorable, however. When photographer Linda Eastman married my old hero, Paul McCartney, in 1969 and joined his band, Wings, people called her an opportunist. And when Yoko Ono married John Lennon and teamed up with him on a couple of albums, it was the same story.

Then there were the wives who got into the stage act in other ways: In 1974, twenty-one-year-old Kathy Silva married rock star Sly Stone in front of 20,000 people at Madison Square Garden; Miss Vicki Budinger married Tiny Tim on *The Tonight Show* in 1969. On the other hand, some rock women have been dragged into the spotlight against their will. In 1979, rock photographer and ex–Bruce Springsteen girlfriend Lynn Goldsmith was snapping pictures of the Boss from the twelfth row in Madison Square Garden when he suddenly spotted her. He charged out into the audience, grabbed her by the arms and hauled her up onstage, where he shouted to the 20,000-strong crowd, "This is my ex-girlfriend!" before flinging her toward the wings.

The Goldsmith incident is mild in comparison with what some rock women have been through. During a drug raid at Rolling Stone Keith Richards's home in England, Mick Jagger's then-girlfriend Marianne Faithfull was discovered by police wearing only a fur rug, the sole woman in the company of eight men. In 1979, Keith Richards's longtime girlfriend, actress Anita Pallenberg, made headlines when the body of a seventeen-year-old boy was found on her unmade bed in Richards's upstate New York mansion. Granted, the incident was disturbing in and of itself (Anita, incidentally, was eventually cleared of having anything to do with the boy's death), but what really shocked me at the time were the pictures of Anita taken as she left court hearings. Where only a few years before, Anita had been lithe and beautiful, now, only in her early thirties, she looked like a frumpy, vastly overweight woman in her late forties. From the looks of things, it seemed to me that life with a rock star could really take its toll on a woman.

I started to wonder about what life was like for other women with rock stars—was it really so great? How does a woman with a rock star contend with a frenzied life-style that has spawned groupies, grueling tours, and excessive amounts of drugs? What does it feel like to have yourself and your relationship under constant public scrutiny? How, in fact, can you even have a normal relationship when the rock star's ego is blown up out of proportion by thousands of worshipful fans? Why do some women and their marriages survive in the rock world while others become drug addicts and divorcees? It was only through interviewing the women closest to some of the biggest influences on popular culture in our time that I found the answers to my questions and more.

For this project, I contacted seventy-two women: ex-wives, current wives, girlfriends, and ex-girlfriends of rock stars from both the past and the present. About one-half of them agreed to be interviewed. Some women—like Jerry Hall and Marianne Faithfull—turned me down because they were in the process of doing their own biographies. Alana Stewart had given a number of interviews to English tabloids following her divorce from Rod Stewart, but by the time I reached her, she turned me down, saying that she felt she had exhausted the subject to death. Cynthia Lennon declined to be interviewed for the same reason. As for my one-time nemesis, Jane Asher, I discovered that in the seventeen years since she and Paul McCartney parted ways, she has refused all interviews. I also found out that today she is happily married to British cartoonist Gerald Scarfe, the mother of three children, still does some acting, and is the author of two how-to books for parents of young children. Some women never bothered to reply at all, but Bianca Jagger called me one morning at 9:30 to tell me that although she didn't want to be interviewed, because she "didn't want to be associated as the wife of someone," nevertheless she thought my project was a "good idea" and was very encouraging. In the course of our conversation, some of my suspicions about the negative aspects of being involved with a rock star were confirmed. "So many of these women allow themselves to be destroyed in the adulation of the male gods," she said. "It's terrible. In the marriage, it's very hard for rock stars to relate to anybody in a normal way, because other women become so available to them."

At times during my search, pinning down the women for an interview proved to be difficult because they never seemed to be in the same place for more than a week. Indeed, Angie Bowie didn't even seem to have a place she called home. Whenever I wanted to get hold of her, I had to leave a message at one of five phone numbers in Los Angeles and New York belonging to various male friends of hers. Sometimes women wouldn't be pinned down even when I finally did get hold of them, as in the case of Anita Pallenberg, who hemmed and hawed for ten months before finally agreeing to an interview. Buddy Holly's widow, Maria Elena Holly Diaz, agreed to talk, but only on the condition that I pay her a $500 "license fee" for the right to use her late husband's name in a commercial publication. Apparently, she instituted this practice after being ripped off a number of times. I sympathized with her plight, but decided to forgo the interview.

In many cases, it was the rock stars themselves who encouraged their women to speak; in one instance, the singer Donovan was not only eager for his wife, Linda, to do the interview, but went so far as to pick me up in their car at the train station in Windsor, England, where they lived. On another occasion, a business consultant hired by Rolling Stone Ron Wood said that part of his job involved getting Ron's wife, Jo, to take a more active part on behalf of her husband. "I see her as being Ron's First Lady," he said.

For this book, I traveled to London; Los Angeles; Atlanta; Portland, Maine; and a number of other cities to meet with the women. The interviews took place in restaurants, publicists' offices, a drag-racing track in California, a clothing store in Georgia, but most frequently in the homes of the stars themselves. The seventeen women (and one man!) who were ultimately chosen to be in this book range in age from twenty-eight to forty-three and are a real cross section: black; white; single; married; divorced; widowed; parents; childless; career women; housewives; well-to-do; just-getting-by; conservative; wild.

In spite of the fact that most of the women I talked to had not gone beyond high school in their education, I found the majority of them to be very intelligent, perceptive, and knowledgeable about what was going on beyond the parameters of the rock world. As for drugs, well, there was not a dilated pupil in sight. In fact, I counted only three women who smoked cigarettes!

In all of the interviews, each person gave a brief personal history and talked about what it's like to live with a rock star, how they coped—or did not cope—with the hazards that come along with the territory (groupies, drugs, and long separations), and how stardom affected their own relationship, identity, and career.

Although there is no one rock wife/companion prototype, I did note some similarities in some of the women's backgrounds: Several had grown up as military brats, who were obliged to move frequently on account of their father's career. It seemed natural to me, then, that they would be attracted to the transient life-style of a rock star, which involves spending months of each year on the road and/or living in a number of different homes in every corner of the world for a few weeks each year.

Also, many of the women had attended strict parochial schools as teenagers, and it seemed to me that their gravitation toward the rock world was a reaction to their upbringing. To them, the rock world looked like a place where there were no restrictions and no rules and they could be free to dream and do as they pleased.

Indeed, parochial school or no, most of the women I spoke with were attracted to the rock-star life-style because they saw it as a ticket to freedom, a world where they could throw away their bras, hitchhike around the country, and be sexually liberated. But it was my observation that once many of these women hooked up with a rock star, they became helpless, overly dependent partners in the most unliberating of relationships. From what I saw and heard, it seems, sadly, that the rock world is still a strong bastion of male chauvinist piggery, in which the women's lives still revolve around their men's. Bianca Jagger agreed. "Of all the worlds, this is really the most male-oriented world that I have encountered in my life," she said. "The competition between women is the most frightening thing."

The most enjoyable part of this project was being able to meet and talk with the women I had heard and read about since I was a child. Even though our lives couldn't be more different, with one or two exceptions, I ended up feeling as comfortable with these women as I do with my own women friends.

While writing this book, some of my impressions of rock wives and companions that I'd carried around with me since I was a little girl were dispelled, whereas others were confirmed. I hope that when you read this book, it will do the same for you.

"Rock and roll wives . . . Aach, I hate 'em. Fortunately, there's only a couple of 'em around, but honestly I don't know how they have the nerve to continue in the face of their appalling failure."

—MICK JAGGER

Myra Lewis

JERRY LEE LEWIS

"The press had a field day with us. Jack Paar said we had a double-ring ceremony—a wedding ring and a teething ring."

*I*n recent years, there has been so much bad press on Jerry Lee Lewis, the wildman singer from the Mississippi Delta who shot to stardom in the fifties pounding out hits like "Great Balls of Fire" and "Whole Lotta Shakin' Goin' On," that people are no longer surprised when they hear about his latest battle with pills, booze, a perforated stomach ulcer, the IRS, and women. (Two of his six wives died under mysterious circumstances: Wife number four drowned in a swimming pool, and wife number five was found dead of a drug overdose in the house she shared with Jerry.)

But back in 1957, in the days when Jerry wasn't walking around under a dark cloud, people were plenty scandalized when he took his thirteen-year-old cousin, Myra Brown, from Memphis as his third wife. Jerry, who had managed to keep the marriage secret for six months, was in England performing to sell-out crowds when the news broke. Headlines in that country screamed, BABY-SNATCHER, and Jerry's tour was canceled. In the United States the reaction to the marriage was just as bad. Jerry's concert dates and television appearances were also canceled, and for the next few years Jerry was hired to perform at only a fraction of the large fees he had once commanded.

But what became of the child bride? As it turned out, Myra was married to Jerry for thirteen years—longer than any of his other wives have managed to stick it out. During that time she did a lot of growing up. She bore him two children: Stevie, who drowned in 1962 at the age of three in the family swimming pool, and Phoebe, now

twenty-one and a photographer in Atlanta. And she had
to contend with a husband who seemed to get meaner with
each year and who got physically and verbally abusive when
he drank. (He once hit her with a plate of spaghetti.) "Under stress and pressure, that little girl died," says Myra
Lewis, now thirty-nine and a realtor in Atlanta. "She just
absolutely gave out and gave up. I know there were good
times, but the bad news took over and destroyed most of
the good news." Myra divorced Jerry in 1970. If there was
one thing that she learned from that marriage, it is, she
says, that she doesn't "ever want to marry anyone famous
ever again!"

∎ ∎ ∎

It is five o'clock in the afternoon on a warm Friday in
March, and Myra Lewis has just returned home—a handsome modern brick house in a well-to-do neighborhood in
Stone Mountain, Georgia—after putting in a full day's work
at the office. Myra, looking much younger than her thirty-
nine years, is still wearing her Century 21 uniform—gold
jacket, brown skirt—and is talking and dashing around her
house at about a hundred miles an hour. "I'm still wound
up from the job," she announces. "You see, I'm a worka-
holic—I work nine days a week, and when I come home,
I'm dyin' to get to the phone!"

Myra may be a working woman, but at times she seems
more like an excitable teenager—cracking jokes, then col-
lapsing in laughter, flirting with the photographer and
screaming when someone calls to tell her she's won a mi-
crowave. "I've got a big case of the sillies," says Myra. "I
just refuse to take everything too seriously. In real estate,
if I have to work with someone who doesn't have a sense
of humor, I'll give 'em to somebody else."

But Myra hasn't always been like this. "When I was
twelve, I was a very old twelve," she says. She is sitting
down—at last!—at her kitchen table and is pulling the crusts

off her turkey sandwich as she talks. "I was very concerned with problems. I had seen this movie about a bomb
coming and just destroying the whole world. At night I
would lay down and think, 'Is this the night the bomb is
going to come? Everything will be destroyed, and this will
be as far as I ever get in life.'

"What I wanted when I was ten, eleven, or twelve years
old was a home, a child, the little white cottage with the
ivy growing around the door, little roses outside, and a little baby sitting in a high chair, and I was horrified that I
would never have it because this horrible bomb was going
to come and wipe it all away."

School was not Myra's finest moment. "It was like, let's
get this show over with—let's get on with something that's
real. I wasn't real popular in school. One year when I was
in the sixth grade, we moved in the middle of the school
year. The girls had this little clique, and all of a sudden I
was the new kid on the block and the word was, 'Don't
talk to her and don't play with her.' And nobody would
come near me. I felt like the ugly duckling. I retreated off
into myself and my own little world."

One evening when Myra was in the seventh grade, her
cousin, Jerry Lee Lewis, came for dinner. He had recorded a song, "Whole Lotta Shakin' Goin' On," and it had
made him a rich and famous rock and roll star, with more
women after him than he could shake a stick at. Nevertheless, the Killer took a shining to his young cousin, Myra.
For the next few months, he brought her gifts and chauf-
feured her to school in his brand-new Eldorado converti-
ble, much to the envy of her classmates. Then, all of
sudden, Jerry suggested to Myra that they get married.
Myra, who'd had it up to here with school, needed only a
few minutes to think it over before she said yes. So, on
December 12, 1957, Jerry, twenty-two, and Myra, thirteen, were married in secret in Hernando, Mississippi. It
took them a few days to work up the nerve to tell her par-

ents, who were, not surprisingly, bewildered and out-
raged. Myra's dad even threatened to take the strap to her.
But as it turned out, Myra was allowed to withdraw from
school and leave home with Jerry. Myra didn't own a suit-
case, so she packed all her belongings in a red cardboard
dollhouse that Santa had given her for Christmas and left
for New York by car with Jerry, who was scheduled to
perform at several sell-out Christmas shows put on by rock
and roll entrepreneur Alan Freed.

Six weeks later they were back in Memphis, house
hunting. "We just wanted an instant house," Myra says.
"We just drove around one Sunday and saw the For Sale
sign up on a house. We went up and knocked on the door,
and Jerry said, 'You're selling this house?' and they said
yes, and we walked in and looked at it and tried to buy
their furniture—their towels, their dishes, everything."

Even though Myra hadn't liked her old life, making the
transition to her new role as housewife was not exactly easy.
"All of a sudden I was removed from one world where I
didn't fit and put into another world where I didn't fit,
either. All of a sudden I had to be in the adult world. I
was thirteen years old and I had to take care of a house,
I had to drive a car, I had to grocery-shop, I had to cook.
I had to do all these things and I didn't know how to do
them. But they were expected of me," laughs Myra heartily. "Jerry had a slot to put me in. He definitely had job
expectations, a job description, so to speak. He had seen
my mother and he thought, 'Now *that's* the kind of wife a
man wants. Always there, good cook, good housekeeper,
takes care of everything. Doesn't fuss and argue and all that
kind of stuff. He's definitely the man of the house, and she's
the woman, and they complement each other.' I had no
problem with that. That was exactly what I wanted to be."

Jerry managed to keep his third marriage a secret from
the world for six months. But the news broke when Jerry
and Myra sailed to England for a major tour and an in-

quisitive reporter managed to worm it out of a chatty,
guileless Myra. Jerry tried to temper the shocking news by
making Myra out to be fifteen instead of thirteen, but it
didn't do any good. "The press," remembers Myra, "had
a field day with us. We just made good copy and scandal."
In particular, she remembers watching Jack Paar taking
potshots at them on his national television show. "He said
we had a double-ring ceremony—a wedding ring and a
teething ring. And have you ever heard of sack dresses?
They said I wore sack diapers. And then the other one was
that Jerry was appearing at the Rue de Paris in New York
and that I'd go see his show and they said, 'Oh, no. Her
bedtime is eight-thirty." Myra laughs about it now, but at
the time she was infuriated by the jokes. "I thought I was
an adult and how dare they insult me? I may have only
been thirteen, but my gosh, my mind must have been
twenty-five!"

In any case, the disclosure of Jerry's marriage was enormously damaging to his career. "Jerry was run out of England, his career was destroyed, his records were pulled off the air," says Myra rather dramatically, sounding like a narrator for a documentary on Jerry's life. "He could not have a TV show because he had married his thirteen-year-old cousin. And he wasn't completely divorced from his second wife." And while Jerry himself never did anything to make Myra feel bad about the damage done to his career ("Even to this day he says, 'I'd do it all over again' "), Myra nonetheless felt extremely guilty. "I felt guilty because they messed up his career. They just about destroyed his name for ten years—the best years of his life. Because he loved me. So therefore somebody had to bear the guilt. So it was me. I felt guilty. So consequently that made me tolerate a lot of bad. When you think bad of yourself, you think, 'Yeah, I *should* be treated bad. I'm a rotten person. I deserve this. I caused all this."

Accordingly, Myra did allow herself to be treated badly, partly out of guilt but also, like many women who lived in the days before women's liberation was a household word, she didn't know any better. "It was the fifties and sixties, and women were subservient to men," she says. "Men were definitely superior—in the Deep South, particularly, it was a male chauvinist pig attitude. Men dominated women. Women had no rights or opinions. It was very unfair. If a man had the slightest bit of a mean streak in him," she says, crossing her arms and legs, "he could really take advantage. Men would slap their wives for sassing them. Now, how can one adult sass another adult? Children get sassy or smart-mouthed to authority, but how is it that the man is the authority over a woman?

"I was married during the generation of the hypocrites. They said, 'Do as I say, not as I do.' Out in the world Jerry could drink and raise hell and everything was fine. But inside our house he did not allow drinking. If you came to our house with a drink, you sat out in your car and fin-

ished it and then came into the house. I never set foot in
a liquor store until I was twenty-six years old."

Jerry had other rules. On the road, he wouldn't allow
Myra to mingle backstage or go to parties with him. "He
didn't want me to see a bunch of drunks following him
around. He wanted me pure and above the world." Myra
will never forget how livid Jerry got the time a man *did*
say, "Damn," in front of her. "Jerry said, 'Hey. You're
talkin' in front of my wife.' He wouldn't let anybody say
anything bad in front of me. I was too overprotected. Jerry
did not want me to be a part of this world, but apart from
the world. He wanted me isolated. He wanted to be able
to walk through the front door and there was an entirely
different world inside of his house. He wanted a little girl
that looked to him for all her advice, and tell her what life
is all about and he'll give you his opinion and that's all you
need to know," sighs Myra. "I had only been an extension
of somebody. I sat at Jerry's feet, brushed his hair or rubbed
his hands and believed everything he told me. Absolutely
worshiped him. I was spoon-fed little portions of life and
told what to think and what to believe, what to feel. Jerry
always said he liked me best in blue jeans and a ponytail,
'cause that's the little girl."

Consequently, Jerry forbade Myra to wear makeup,
jewelry, or fashionable clothes. In the company of other
women, Myra felt "like a bar of homemade soap." Especially around someone like Priscilla Presley, whom Myra
used to see at her beauty parlor in Memphis. "Priscilla was
always so pretty, so striking," Myra remembers. "A totally different kind of pretty than she is today. She had
the dyed black hair with the false eyelashes and the artifi-
cial makeup look. She was glamorous, she was photo-
graphed all the time, she looked beautiful, and here I felt
like a dishrag. If I saw Priscilla comin', I would hide. The
girl followed me home one day from the beauty shop, actually got in the car and followed me all the way home.

When I drove up my driveway, I rushed into my house so I wouldn't see her. It wasn't because I didn't want to know her. It was because I was too intimidated by her." Then there is a tiny pause in the conversation while Myra takes out a tube of lip gloss from her purse and quickly runs it over her lips. When she resumes speaking, she says she regrets that she wasn't more receptive to Priscilla's overtures. "If I hadn't been so insecure and afraid of being around Priscilla because she was such an attractive woman, she and I would have had more in common than any two women on the face of the earth."

It was not until she had been married for a good ten years that Myra discovered that there were women in the world who thought for themselves. "When I was about twenty-three years old, I had a next-door neighbor that I went over one day and met, and she had this outgoing, bubbly personality and she had thoughts all her own. She didn't have to have a thought that was only duplicated because her husband told her to think about it. And I was fascinated." Myra's voice drops to a whisper. "I said, 'My God, there are people who walk around and think for themselves.' It's been fifteen years since I've seen her, but she had an impact on my life, and I know she doesn't have the foggiest idea. But it was a little seed planted in me, a 'Hey, maybe I do have an opinion. Maybe I am a complete, whole person. Maybe what Jerry says isn't one hundred percent right.' You know," Myra says sheepishly, "there was a point when he could have told me that black was white and I'd have fought the world and said, 'Black is white.' "

So when Myra started to grow up a little and think on her own, Jerry tried to squelch her. When she began to threaten to leave him over his treatment of her, he'd tell her she was ugly—"No Liz Taylor," he'd say. "You better come back, because nobody else is gonna want *you*."

Although his words cut her to the quick then, Myra says that in going back in her mind over those years with him

she can now understand why he said those things. Tears
well up in her eyes as she attempts to explain his motives:
"Jerry said those things because he loved me and he wanted
to keep me." There is a long pause while Myra tries in vain
to blink back the tears. "He wanted to preserve that little
girl that he loved," she sobs, "and he was willing to destroy me to do that."

If that was the case, how did she escape him before he
totally destroyed her?

The decision to leave, it seems, came after a particularly
unsettling evening when Jerry had called Myra several times
from the road in the middle of the night, screaming ob-
scenities and accusing her of being a whore. While Jerry
was still on the phone, Myra reached into a drawer, pulled
out a pistol, put it to her head, and told Jerry that she was
going to kill herself.

"I had reached a point," she says. "There was no continuing. There was no more tolerating it and being miserable. It was either die or leave. Because when I put the
gun to my head and seriously considered puttin' an end to
it and I realized how close I was to meetin' up with that
bullet and I said"—Myra's voice lowers to a whisper again—
" 'No. No. This can't be right.' I guess the biggest threat,
and a lot of men will use this on women, 'Well, you can
leave, but you're gonna leave the kids here.' He always told
me, 'If you want to leave, hit the road. Go ahead. But
Phoebe stays.' He knew I wasn't going anywhere without
Phoebe. And I thought I'd have to leave without her. Until that night when I said, 'Wait a minute. I am leavin' and
I am takin' Phoebe. And I'll kill anybody who tries to stop
me.' I became dangerous then, because I was fightin' for
my life and was fightin' for my child's life." So Myra
snatched up Phoebe and fled. And in 1970, Myra and Jerry
were divorced. Shortly after the divorce, Myra married a
man named Pete Malito, whom she had met when she hired
him to follow Jerry, in order to surprise him in an act of

infidelity. That marriage lasted three years. Marrying Pete, was, in her words, "an act of desperation, an act of revenge, an act of stupidity. None of it was for the right reasons. The only thing good that came out of it was that it got me out of Memphis and got me to Atlanta, where I could be somebody other than the ex-wife of Jerry Lee Lewis."

After her second divorce, Myra was not very receptive to men. "I had this extremely bitter feeling because when I divorced Pete, I got mad at Jerry all over again. Because he was the reason I married that fool! So I did not want a relationship."

So Myra concentrated on getting a job instead. In Atlanta, Myra got a ninety-three-dollar-a-week job as a receptionist at a floral-distribution warehouse. (Myra had acquired a few business skills from the business school she'd attended while she was still married to Jerry. She'd gone on the sly because he didn't want her there. "His reasoning was, 'You don't need an education to scrub the kitchen floors and have babies,' " says Myra.) Then, at the suggestion of her father, Myra got her realtor's license and got a job at Century 21. The work was right up her alley. She brags, "Just tell me about a piece of land. Give me the dimensions on it, give me the zoning requirements, give me the lay of the land, the topography, and I carry it right here," she says pointing to her head.

The work was not the only thing that Myra found to her liking at Century 21: For the last three years, she has been steadily dating her boss there ("It's no secret"). Myra pops up from the table and brings back a photo of her guy. From the picture, he looks like a friendly bear of a man who might very well do some taking care of Myra. When this is suggested to her, Myra says, "Oh, yeah. It's nothing like with Jerry. I mean, he's considerate, he is conscientious of what I want, my needs and desires. With Jerry, it was an unconditional love. I loved him regardless of how

Myra Lewis in her work clothes.

he treated me or whether I felt the love returned back to me."

At this point, the front door bangs, and Phoebe Lewis, blond and willowy and twenty-one, breezes into Myra's kitchen and heads straight for the fridge. With Phoebe around, Myra's already-excitable voice reaches a positively feverish pitch. Together, Myra and her daughter act more like sisters, exchanging good-natured insults and telling each other in detail about each of their latest junk-food binges. At one point, Myra makes an unsuccessful grab at Phoebe to take her hair out of its ponytail so that everybody can see how beautiful it is (Phoebe, it seems, has inherited her daddy's silken locks). When Phoebe leaves, armed with a bag of Hershey's kisses Myra had bought especially for her, Myra confides, "When Phoebe hit thirteen, I sweated that whole year. I looked at her and thought, 'Oh, my God,' 'cause that's when I knew what I'd done to my parents. I was a mother twice when I was Phoebe's age. I buried my son when I should have been graduating from high school." When Phoebe herself was in high school, she had very little in common with the kids her age because, says Myra, "she had been through the trauma of that other daddy. She has seen her daddy dragged through every kind of scandal you can imagine. She would see her daddy with these girls that were crazy dope addicts or whatever. One time her daddy picked her up at the airport along with his girl-friend. He passed out in the car. Phoebe had to give him mouth-to-mouth resuscitation to keep him alive till they got to the hospital. Now," Myra leans forward in her chair, "when you've done that and you go to school and these little girls were concerned with the color of the mascara they wore and 'Tommy didn't call me.' Big deal. Every-thing was so anticlimactic that she didn't want anything to do with it. It's the measuring stick of what is a problem."

Phoebe is one of the few people that gets that "soft flow" from Jerry. Myra herself is another. Myra explains: "I'm one of the few people who can unruffle his feathers. With Jerry, he can be in a room full of people and I cannot be there and he is mad and he is stomping and he is raving and he has cussed about three people out and there's about four people sittin' in the corner afraid to open their mouths. They're sittin' there goin', 'I ain't gonna say a word or he will get up and hit me.' And he would! He can be just that mean and just that mad and I can come in the room and just go over and look at him and just kind of stare him down a second. I call him Daddy. And I look at him and I say, 'Daddy, why are you being so mean?' And he'll just look at me and go, 'Don't you give me a hard time.' Then I'll talk soft to him, almost like talkin' to a baby, and he'll go, 'You don't know these stupid people like I do.' And I'll say, 'Don't worry about it, just let it go.' And he'll go, 'Well, OK.' And he'll just mellow out. He'll just get easy and soft and he'll be nice.

"See," Myra continues, "I was the only stabilizing force in Jerry's life. From that point on it was just chaos. Everyone that's walked into Jerry's life has either become a tragedy, a fatality, or a disruption. None of them have had any stabilizing force. I was always the calm, sedate, I'll-take-care-of-it, I'll make the decision, there's nothing to worry about, I got both hands on the wheel. And I always projected that image to him and that's what he got from me."

Since Myra, there have been three more wives in Jerry's life. After Myra came Jaren, who would end up drowning while waiting for a divorce decree from Jerry (she had accused him of threatening her life). When she was alive and still married to Jerry, she used to call Myra from time to time and ask her to go back to Jerry. "She said, 'Myra, he doesn't love me. He's just trying to replace you. Won't you please go back to him?' Then she'd call and ask me for recipes. 'Myra, how did you fix that beef stew? All he can talk about is 'I want some of Myra's beef stew.' See," Myra goes on to explain, "after I left, Jerry's life-style got worse.

His drug problem got worse. His drinking got worse. He got meaner. So therefore he made the women in his life have a worse life. Jaren had it bad. But Shawn [Shawn Lewis, wife number five, who died mysteriously in 1983, barely three months after her marriage to Jerry] had it worse."

Myra may be the only person left in America who doesn't think that Jerry was responsible in one way or another for Shawn's death, as it has been hinted at so broadly in the press. She has this to say on the subject: "Once again, I think the press is on a witch-hunt looking for someone to hang, and they've got them a nice candidate. Jerry's not guilty. He didn't kill that girl. He didn't shove pills down her throat or do any of those outrageous things. He was too drugged up himself!" She shakes her head. "It surpasses absurd after a while."

What Jerry really needs in his life right now is a nice woman, says Myra. (Since this interview took place, Jerry took twenty-two-year-old Kerrie McCarver as bride number six. As of this writing they are still together.) "But I don't think a nice woman could live with him. Where's he going to meet one? His attitude is the majority of them are sluts, 'cause that's all he ever sees." And even if he did find a nice woman, "Why's she going to stay in there? Is she going to go in there and clean up?"

Jerry's biggest problem, as it has been for years, says Myra, is his hellfire-and-brimstone religion—Church of God Pentecostal. "The religion that he had me indoctrinated into will give you a hundred quick ways to get to hell. They made him believe you can't live what you believe. If you have an evil thought, you're evil. And if you're evil, you're going to hell. Whatever happened to 'God is love' and peace for mankind and love for one another? There wasn't any of that. It was guilt. It was 'Don't go to the movies because if you do, you go to hell.' 'Don't wear diamonds 'cause it's a sin.' 'Jezebel painted her face, so don't put makeup

on.' It's a shame. The man is tortured. Jerry thinks that
Jerry is too wicked to be saved.

"I don't think Jerry's grown up yet," she continues. "Jerry
is still very much of a little confused bad little boy. He is
very undisciplined. He's mean. He's spoiled. He's a little
boy who's been ravaged by disaster. He's lost everything
that's meant anything to him. He's got two sons dead, a
mother and father dead, two wives dead. The only thing
he's got is Phoebe and his music. The fact that he can sit
down and play at that piano, that's his escape." Myra sighs.
"And it's made him somewhat bitter and hard and resent-
ful."

Nevertheless, their relationship today is amicable. "God,
I'd fight a circus off of Jerry," she declares. "I'd love to see
him sell fifty billion trillion records. The way I figure it,
if I could walk away from a relationship of that duration
and not care whether he lives or dies, being the father of
my children, then I'm no better than the animals out there.
Most women end up with a hate for somebody who tries
to destroy them or for someone who mistreats them. But
how can I hate somebody who loved me that much? There
were years when I was torn. I hated him and felt guilty. I
used to dream . . . when I left Jerry, I felt like I had
abandoned a two-year-old child in the middle of a free-
way. I felt like I had tossed him out to the wolves. I had
nightmares for five years. I would see him standin' there
cryin', begging me to come back."

And what does Jerry think of the new liberated Myra?
Myra smiles, "On a good day, he will brag on me and he
will say, 'That's one of the finest people you'll ever meet.
She took my daughter and raised her good. She put her
through school and she's done that.' And then he'll say,
'Dad-gone I couldn't get that woman to come back to me.
Why wouldn't she come back and give me another
chance?' "

Lee Angel

LITTLE RICHARD

"I'm the woman that Richard wanted to be."

*W*hen Little Richard burst onto the rock-and-roll scene with "Tutti-Frutti" in 1955, no one had ever seen or heard anything like him: He sang in a whooping, shouting falsetto and wore his hair high in a pompadour and sported mascara and pancake makeup. Offstage, his sexual preference was anyone's guess. Still, audiences loved him, and "Tutti-Frutti" and other records that followed sold by the millions.

Suddenly, at the height of his career, Little Richard decided to chuck fame and fortune as a rock star for the serener pastures of the ministry. For several years, Little Richard Penniman preached in the Seventh Day Adventist Church. In 1964, he returned to rock and roll, but he was never able to re-create his earlier success. Nevertheless, his influence on rock music has been incalculable and has inspired countless present-day musicians—David Bowie, Mick Jagger, and Paul McCartney, to name just a few.

Audrey Sherbourne, a voluptuous former stripper who performed in the fifties and sixties under the name Lee Angel—is one woman who has known Little Richard through all of his metamorphoses. At one point, Audrey claims, she and Richard were so close that they were planning to marry. But she walked out on him—supposedly on the day they had set for the wedding. Nevertheless, until very recently, she and Little Richard remained on good terms. In Little Richard's recently published autobiography, Audrey/Lee Angel figures quite prominently and colorfully.

■ ■ ■

Lee Angel is in a little bit of a huff. She has caught that devil of a Little Richard spreading stories about her again—this time in an interview he did for the *Valleydale News*. She grabs the incriminating evidence from a drawer and skims the article quickly, every so often tsk-tsking over something Richard has said about her. The one item, it seems, that particularly gets her goat is when Richard is quoted as saying that Angel told him that she was going to sue him because he made her look "loose" in his autobiography. "If I'm going to sue you," Angel says, addressing an imaginary Richard next to her, "I'm not going to call you and tell you I'm going to sue you. The first time you know I'm going to sue you is when you get the papers in your hands."

Angel laughs, in spite of herself. No matter how worked up she may appear to be over Little Richard's "lies" about her, it seems pretty obvious that Angel likes all the attention. Since she quit stripping several years ago ("There are no decent clubs for me to work in anymore. What they're asking me to do onstage, I wouldn't do in the privacy of my own bedroom"), life has been pretty quiet. She found work as a house renovator; most nights she plays pinochle with a next-door neighbor. Then Little Richard's book came out, and since then Angel has been asked to do print and television interviews. She enjoys having her neighbors say things such as that they saw her on a local Los Angeles talk show, although Angel professes to be a little annoyed about how things turned out on that program. "They called me a groupie or some shit like that," she says. "*That's* the pitch Richard's been giving me. But, honey, I went around the world as a stripper. I've headlined in other countries and I have a pretty good following myself."

Angel and Richard met in 1956, back when Lee was still plain old Audrey Sherbourne and a sixteen-year-old high school student in Savannah, Georgia. Dressed in pedal pushers and her father's best white shirt, Angel was on her

way to the soda parlor with a bunch of friends from school
when Richard, who was in town for a concert, spied her
from his hotel window. "I remember one of my classmates
ran over to me and said, 'Hey! Little Richard wants to see
you!' " (Richard, in his biography, says he was attracted
to Lee's voluptuous figure "a fifty-inch bust and eighteen-
inch waist," but Angel claims that the measurements are
grossly exaggerated: "My tits are only forty-Double-D
now—when I was sixteen years old, I was wearing a thirty-
two-B bra.")

At any rate, Lee had never seen Richard in concert, although she had certainly heard some outrageous stories
about him. "I grew up around show business. My parents
used to be members of a society that used to bring all the
black entertainers into Savannah. So I already knew people like Johnny Ace, Guitar Slim. My stepmom was the
best cook in the country, and everybody liked to come to
her house and eat when they were in town, so that's how
I grew up around these people. So naturally I heard the
rumors about Richard—that he was strange," she says, to
use a euphemism. (Somehow, Angel can't seem to use the
word *gay* in reference to Richard.)

"But my friends told me to go on up and meet him. And
I went up to his hotel room and I walked in the door and
I took one look at him and . . . Yuk! I don't know what
happened. I was plagued for the rest of my life. The moment I saw him, I heard bells ring, I got dizzy. He was
lying on the bed." At this stage in his life, she says, "Richard hadn't gotten into the makeup. He did dress a little
wild and he always kept his hair pretty. I've always been
the direct type. 'You want to see me?' I said. 'I'm a girl!' "
Angel chuckles for a while at the memory. "He said he knew
and he wanted to know if I was coming to his concert that
night. I had no intentions of going to Little Richard's concert that night. When I left home, that was the last thing
on earth that I wanted to get close to." But she ended up

agreeing to go. "When I left him, I ran out of the place and I ran down to my dad's garage and asked him for some money for new shoes and a dress. Daddy said, 'What? What? What?' And I said, 'Oh, I'm going to see Little Richard tonight.' And my father said, '*You* are going to see Little Richard? I thought you didn't like Little Richard.' " But she talked her dad into giving her the money for her first pair of high-heeled shoes and a dress. That night, after the concert, she stayed out with Richard until two o'clock in the morning—the latest she'd ever stayed out on a date. Apparently, they got along well that night. "It was flirt, pretty flirt, pretty," she remembers.

The day after their date, Richard left Savannah for his next stop on the tour. Angel did not see him again until after she had graduated from high school and was living with an aunt in Philadelphia and working in little clubs as a dancer. "Then I heard that Richard was going to be in Wilmington, Delaware. So I went to Wilmington. Richard was happy to see me, I was happy to see Richard, and that's when my life changed. The next thing I knew, I woke up in Washington, D.C. I got drunk for the first time in my life. Only I didn't get me drunk; Richard got me drunk. I always remember waking up the next morning and the first thing I realized that there was a man next to me. And then I opened my eyes and I did not know where I was. And I want to turn over, but I don't want to wake up this man over here. But I want to see who this man is. And it must have taken me three hours to inch my way over, to turn over and keep from waking up whoever was in bed with me until I find out who it was. And it was Richard! And that was the beginning of the relationship."

For the next year and a half, Angel traveled on the road with Richard whenever she could. Sometimes Richard arranged it so that she could work on the road, too. "He had me put on a show with Ray Charles and Bob and Ray and Mickey and Sylvia—only the people he trusted. I'd be the

opening or middle act." When Angel wasn't on the road, she was still living with her aunt in Philly. "Sometimes Richard would call there, and my aunt would say, 'Well, she just went to the store to get a loaf of bread for me.' And he would go off. He'd get mad and angry and pissed. And I would come back, and my aunt would always scream the same thing: 'Call that madman! Call that madman!' "

Even when Angel and Richard were separated, they could still communicate telepathically, she says. "He could be anywhere on earth and if I really missed him, I could just sit down and concentrate on Richard and Richard would call me within half an hour." And if they went too long without seeing each other, she says, "Richard would start going crazy. Then the boys would start talking about me." They knew that if he called up Angel and asked her to come visit for a while, "that would be the only time he acted human, and not only would he act human, he was tranquil for weeks after. When I'd go back home, they'd have a nice, calm Richard on their hands."

One of the things that upsets Angel about Richard's book, she says, is that he "hasn't mentioned any of the beauty of our relationship. We mostly used to talk about us, about 'When you're forty, I want you to look this way,' and saying how beautiful our life is going to be twenty-five years from now. We used to have what was I guess the only normal relationship Richard's ever had in his life."

Life on the road with Little Richard was "wild," says Angel. They snatched sleep whenever and wherever they could: Angel remembers one time sleeping in a projection room in a theater, right under the speakers. As for dining conditions, they ate on what was known as the "chitlin' circuit"—that is, greasy spoons patronized by blacks only. "In those places, if you didn't buy the roaches a steak, you didn't eat in peace. And that was all that was open to blacks in those days—even for a star like Little Richard or Chuck Berry or Fats Domino." At one point, she remembers, when everyone was sick and tired of eating in those places, Little

Richard talked Angel, who is a very light-skinned black, into going into a White Castle and trying to pass herself off as white. "They parked around the corner, and I walked in. I'm nervous. It scared me. Here I'm a little girl, twelve o'clock at night and I just walked in with all these white people. I ordered twenty hamburgers and nobody paid any attention to me, but it took me a long time before I could relax with doing it."

Angel has many fond memories of the road, but certainly the most memorable one has to be the time that Richard introduced Angel to his audience at a show at Chicago's Old Civic Opera House. "Richard told the world that he was going to marry me. He introduced me to fifty thousand people in one night as his fiancée, and that night as we were leaving the auditorium the kids came up and ripped my dress off, and here I was standing in the middle of Chicago with nylon stockings, panties, and garter belt."

In his book, Richard denies that he ever asked Angel to marry him, but Angel says that's just Richard making up stories again. As she tells it, they had even set a date for the wedding: September 1, 1957. But instead of walking up the aisle on that day, Angel walked out on him. Richard was getting "funny" ideas about what he wanted her to do, she says. "He was starting to get kinky and things of that nature. He was trying to get me to play with people and people to play with me. A good example is the Buddy Holly story [in his book, Richard describes how he watched Angel having sex with Buddy Holly backstage]. In the beginning, it was just watching, and then it got to be me participating, and that's when I drew the line. He'd get somebody and he'd say, 'C'mon baby, do it, do it. Please me.' That just wasn't me. He didn't want to respect the fact that 'Hey, sorry, I'm not into doing this.' So I ran. I vanished. Everybody was surprised, but if there's something I'm uncomfortable doing, I don't do it. And believe me, I'm no angel!"

Why did Richard want her to do all these things? Well,

Angel has it figured out this way: "You see, I'm the woman that Richard wanted to be. I am Little Richard's alter-ego. When he used to have his parties, when he became the girl, it was me. In his fantasies he became me."

Except on one occasion, Angel did not see Richard again until 1958, after he had renounced rock and roll in favor of a religious calling. "I ran into him when he was preaching in Washington, D.C. I had to go see him. I walked into the church and . . . Richard always knew when I walked into a place. And I watched the whole thing, and suddenly he motioned to one of the deacons and reached in his pocket and gave him something and whispered something. The next thing I knew the guy was standing next to me saying, 'Reverend Penniman says please wait for him in the gold Cadillac outside.' " That was the first time that Angel met Ernestine Campbell, Richard's straightlaced wife, whom he had met at a religious meeting. That day, Richard dropped Ernestine off at their house, and then he and Angel went on over to a friend's house. It was there that Angel discovered that in spite of Richard's new vocation, he was acting like the same old Richard, "trying to get me to play with people and things of that nature." So she walked away from him again. "I knew my presence around him was no good, because he was supposed to be a minister."

Angel would not see Richard again until 1964. In the interim, she was doing quite well in her career as a dancer and stripper and had even ventured into modeling. "I did an assignment for the Nudist Association of America and I had this blanket and they couldn't get me out of this blanket. I am the big stripper, right? And they couldn't get me out of this blanket!"

Her love life wasn't so bad, either. Her first boyfriend after Little Richard was singer Jackie Wilson. "He was totally insane!" shrieks Angel. "Jackie had my door kicked in in Washington, D.C., at the hotel I was staying at, my being kidnapped out of the hotel room, thrown into Cadillacs, soaking wet hair, a very light pair of pajamas on and snow!" As Angel recounts the details she sounds like she's enjoying the scene all over again. "Jackie," she says matter of factly, "was a cocksman. Jackie would go to bed with anything that was young enough or old enough. If you could pull down your panties and pull up your dress, you could be had by Jackie. And Jackie was the first one I met who had a true coke habit."

So life for Angel was going pretty well without Richard. It was not until 1970, while on a tour of Europe, that she decided that she wanted to make contact with him again. "What happened was I was in London and I was watching *The Tom Jones Show*, and it was an episode that Richard was in. He was doing 'A Kiss Is Just a Kiss, A Sigh Is Still a Sigh,' and I saw the loneliest man on earth. I didn't see the makeup and I didn't see the hair, but I did see a friend calling for help, and that's when I came back to the States." She was in for quite a shock. "You should have seen cute little me coming back to the United States after three years in Europe and start looking for Richard. And all my friends told me the same thing, Brook Benton, Johnny Nash, Henry Nash, who was Richard's manager, they all told me the same thing: 'Don't get in touch with Richard. He's going to hurt you. You just don't know Richard. Richard's changed.' And I didn't listen. Richard found me. Richard told me to fly to LA. I did. Oh, Lord," she giggles. "Why hadn't he sent me a round-trip ticket? I'm at the airport, and this was during the tie-dye with the Indian beads and fringe. And I had on a beautiful pirate-purple puff-sleeved see-through blouse. And this limousine pulls up, and seventeen people that I would not want to get caught in a dark alley with got out. Then Little Richard got out." Angel could not believe her eyes. "The makeup, the wig, this is twelve o'clock in the afternoon and he's got on a red-and-gold batwing outfit. He got out of the car, and I right away shut up and I had to get in the limousine with him." At that point, Angel swears that if she'd had a round-trip ticket, she would have disappeared and never be heard from again. "For one thing, the people around him were treating me like a groupie. They would just not let Richard and me get close. Whenever I would get any touch of human being out of him, somebody would start something. And if I got close, they'd probably be out of the picture. And I'd say to Richard, 'Why are you permitting these people to do this to me? Why aren't you defending me?' "

Most likely, Angel feels, Richard's drastic personality change was a result of the number of drugs he was taking. The fact that he was doing drugs at all was a big shock to her.

"Back in '56, '57, Richard didn't drink, Richard didn't smoke, Richard didn't do drugs. He's totally different now." And it was the people around Richard, Angel feels, that were "keeping him in cocaine."

As far as Angel is concerned, ever since that time, Richard hasn't been his old self. "He went into the Twilight Zone and never returned." Still, she keeps on fairly good terms with him, going to stay with him and his mother in Riverside, California, every Christmas. "For Christmas in '79 he gave me a beautiful bible. And it said, 'To my wonderful lady and friend.' "

Even so, Angel knows that she and Richard will never be as close as they once were. "I keep hoping I can trust him, but I know better, so I'm not going to waste my time. I have my own private life and I'm really happy with it." As for Richard, well, in spite of being a minister once more, she says he's regressing back into his old bad self. "He's saying one thing in public and doing another thing in private.

"I'm so happy I never married that man," she says now. "Though I often wonder what would have happened if Richard and I had gotten married. Would one of us be dead by now?"

*S*usan Rotolo

BOB DYLAN

"We kept to ourselves. He would never want anybody to come over, and I would acquiesce to all of that. He made me more paranoid and distrustful."

7he cover photo of Bob Dylan's second album, *Free-wheelin' Bob Dylan*, the 1963 album that would finally establish him as a songwriter, shows a very youthful Dylan strolling down West Fourth Street arm-in-arm with a smiling woman. The woman is lovely-looking, but she is not, as some might think, just a hired model. Her name is Susan Rotolo, and at the time that picture was taken, she was Bob Dylan's nineteen-year-old real-life girlfriend.

When Susan met Dylan in 1961 in New York, he was certainly no star: He was just a scruffy new kid in town who was not even being paid for his appearances at Gerde's Folk City Monday night hootenannies. Yet, as a performer, he stood out even then, remembers Susan. "He was charismatic. Even though he was one of the imitators of Woody Guthrie, he had something of his own."

Susan witnessed the phenomenon of Dylan's growing fame firsthand: She was there when Dylan was singled out in a review in 1961 by *New York Times* folk-music critic Robert Shelton as being, "a bright new face in folk music . . . one of the most distinctive stylists to play in a Manhattan cabaret in months" and was with Dylan when his car was mobbed by hundreds of fans after his triumphant Carnegie Hall concert in 1963. As well, Susan Rotolo was the inspiration for many of Dylan's early songs, including "Boots of Spanish Leather," "Don't Think Twice, It's All Right," and "Tomorrow Is a Long Time."

As Dylan grew more famous, Susan discovered that the fame was affecting their relationship in negative ways, and they parted in 1964. Susan spent the first few years after the breakup trying to hide from fanatic Dylan fans. Fortunately, enough years have gone by for Susan to feel comfortable with talking about what life was like with Dylan in those days: "It's history now," she says. Today, Susan lives in New York with her husband, a film editor, and their five-year-old son. She works as a free-lance illustrator.

■ ■ ■

Susan Rotolo sits cross-legged on a couch in her bright SoHo loft and smiles. It's amazing how little she's changed in appearance in the twenty-one years since she appeared on the cover of *Freewheelin' Bob Dylan*. When this observation is presented to her, she says shyly that she and her son were walking through Tower Records the other day and that she had seen the album out on display. "Just for fun I said, 'Do you know who that is in that picture?' And he looks real carefully and he looks at me and he said, 'That's you, Mommy.' It was cute."

Lucky for Susan's son, Susan is teaching him all of the folk songs that her Italian-American music-loving parents taught her when she was a little girl: "Pete Seeger and Woody Guthrie and Leadbelly—they were all part of the music in our home while we were growing up," says Susan.

As well as getting a solid education in music (and not only folk but classical, opera, jazz, and blues), Susan and her older sister, Carla, were taught by their parents to be politically aware. "This was the fifties. That was the McCarthy era. Teachers, especially, were losing their jobs if they did anything out of the ordinary, so it took courage to do any kind of speaking out at all. I was involved with an organization called SANE—for a Sane Nuclear Policy. I got into trouble in high school because I tried to collect signatures on a petition to ban the bomb. Those were the days of the loyalty oaths. Even students had to sign in order to graduate. I remember agreeing to sign, since I really had no choice, but I wrote "under protest" under my signature. I was taught the value of our Bill of Rights and the Constitution. To have to sign an oath of loyalty to God and country was against one's civil rights."

Because of her political activities and interest in folk music, Susan always felt like a bit of an outsider in high school. "I didn't have too many friends. I was considered too weird. My idols were Edna St. Vincent Millay and Lord Byron, poets instead of movie stars." So she began to hang out with kids from other high schools "who were like me, who were not part of the mainstream, who were socially conscious the way I was. We picketed Woolworth stores here in New York City in conjunction with those in the South who were fighting to integrate the lunch counters at the Woolworth stores there. We were a bunch of young idealistic kids. It was black and white and everything. We were under no danger in New York, but the people in the South were putting their lives on the line."

On Sundays, Susan and her friends would congregate in Washington Square Park to listen to the likes of Woody Guthrie, Jack Elliott, and Pete Seeger play—"a lovely atmosphere for a fourteen-year-old kid," Susan says with a delightful smile. Then, when Susan and her friends got to be a little older, they started going to the hootenannies at Gerde's Folk City. In those days, she says that her and her friends' activities were pretty tame by today's standards. "There were no drugs. Nobody really drank. So it was easier for a mother then to let the kid go out than it is now, when there are drugs and all kinds of things."

For Susan at seventeen, there were few restrictions anyway. "My father died when I was fourteen, and after my father died, my mother was kind of rocky, and both Carla and I had to fend for ourselves in many ways. Then my mother and I were in a car accident and we were both badly injured. Friends of the family took us in . . . me in one place, she in another. As I recovered I was more and more on my own and that was the beginning of my independence at seventeen, when I still really needed some kind of guidance."

College was not a possibility for Susan: "When my father died, I was in my last year of high school and I didn't do well anymore, so my grades were in no shape for a scholarship, and economically there was no way. It's a shame," she muses. "My own doing and life's doing." And although Susan was artistically talented, she says she wasn't "pushed in any way to decide on a career—which was a mistake, I think. So I had a tendency to float along with things."

In the summer after she graduated from high school, Susan worked at odd jobs, waitressing, working at the five-and-dime, and in the evenings going as often as she could to hootenannies and folk concerts at Carnegie Hall and other places to hear people like Pete Seeger, Ewan MacColl, Odetta, Tom Lehrer (a Harvard professor who wrote satirical songs) and others. A friend took her to Gerde's Folk City where Judy Collins, Dave Van Ronk, Carolyn Hester, Peter Yarrow (before he became part of Peter, Paul, and Mary) and many, many others, sang. One of the most popular events at Gerde's there in that summer of '61 was the Monday night hootenannies—"Anyone could get up and play," remembers Susan. It was at one of these hootenannies that Susan first laid eyes on Bob Dylan. "He would play with some guy called Mark Spoelstra. And Mark Spoelstra had lovely shoulders. I thought, 'God, who's that guy with the nice set of shoulders?' " But it was Dylan's harmonica-playing that ultimately proved to be more of a magnet than Spoelstra's shoulders. "I'm a sucker for anyone who plays a good harp," she says—and has been ever since as a child she heard and loved the recordings of a black blues harmonica player named Sonny Terry. "So that was the jump. When I met Dylan, what I loved about him was the way he played the harmonica, I loved that sound. He played with an earthiness that was wonderful."

In Dylan's performances, in those early days, Susan also remembers that there was "a clowniness, a funniness about him. He used to clown around onstage tuning his guitar. He didn't cut the strings, so he would say, 'This guitar needs a haircut.' He was funny. He had an impish kind of personality, like Harpo Marx."

After his performances, Dylan would mingle with the audience ("He was just folks then," says Susan), and sometimes he and Susan would talk. Right from the start, she noticed that there was "an enormous ambition in him, 'cause he had even said he was going to be very big. I took it seriously at the moment, but I had no idea what it meant. *He* didn't know what it meant, he couldn't know then what fame of that magnitude could do to his life."

From time to time, Susan and Dylan would run into each other at parties. At a get-together after a day-long hootenanny at Riverside Church in July, at which Dylan had performed, Susan remembers, "I really got to know Dylan more. We were kind of flirting with each other." She blushes, as if it had all happened yesterday. Then, it seems, after that, all of a sudden they were a couple. "We were working our way into what was to become a serious romance. We were young and vulnerable. A lot of crazy things happened. It is strange to think that so much is made of us together in those years. It could have run its course naturally, but it was shaded and formed by all these outside influences, because of his growing fame."

Susan and Dylan had been going together only a few months when *New York Times* folk-music critic Robert Shelton wrote his now-famous glowing review of Dylan in September 1961. From that point on, Susan remembers, Dylan looked at himself differently. "He was touched by the establishment. He got a review." His friends looked at him differently too. "A lot of people were glad for him.

But there was a lot of envy, I'm sure. Everything began to change."

By the time Dylan had signed his first record deal with Columbia a few months later, Susan could see that he was becoming more and more wrapped up in his career. "His ambition became more synthesized," she says. "Then he began snubbing his old friends. But it was all so understandable in an odd way. He could see these things happening to him and he wanted to make sure they would happen, so at the same time he didn't have time to just hang out anymore. He was working on his image and his career."

And Dylan was working *very* hard at creating just the right image: This involved manufacturing a mythical background for himself about being an orphan from New Mexico who had lived on the road for a long time and going to great lengths to hide the fact that he was really Robert Allan Zimmerman from a middle-class Jewish family in Hibbing, Minnesota. In Susan's opinion, all this hiding from his real background made Dylan "paranoid." "I guess he was paranoid of anybody saying, 'I know who you really are.' "

If some people, at least for a while, believed Dylan's invented stories about himself, right from the beginning Susan's mother did not. "She was smart. I think she knew right away that his name wasn't really Dylan or she could sense, 'Oh, this is some kid from somewhere putting on a whole story.' And by the time I was going out with Dylan, neither she nor Carla really approved of him at all." In fact, Susan's mother's nickname for Dylan was "Twerp."

Eventually, Susan and Dylan took an apartment together on West Fourth Street. As a couple, Susan remembers that they could be very "exclusive. We'd always be huddled together or holding hands or arm-in-arm. In *many* ways, we kept to ourselves. He would never want anybody to come over, he would never want anybody to be around. I don't think I really liked it that much, 'cause I'm the kind who is very trustful of people usually, but I would acquiesce to all of that." As a result of his paranoia, she says, "He made *me* more paranoid and distrustful. You take on somebody you're with, their traits, you live the man's life. What a shame," she says, shaking her head.

While Dylan was working on his career and becoming more famous by the hour, Susan, in addition to her odd jobs, was doing the scenery for a series of off-Broadway plays. One production was *Brecht on Brecht* at the Circle in the Square, then located on Sheridan Square in the Village. She loved the work. "Bertolt Brecht was someone who influenced me enormously at that time, so naturally I shared that with Bob," she says. "Brecht was a Communist and he chose to live in East Germany, knowing full well how difficult it would be to survive as an artist in such a rigid society. This man was in terrible conflict. He couldn't live in the East or the West. In those years I was fascinated by that and through Brecht's works I tried to understand how he resolved that dilemma."

As she got older, Susan still maintained her sense of idealism. "I had a strong sense of injustice of the world and rectifying that injustice." These beliefs prompted her to take a job with CORE (Congress for Racial Equality). "It was essentially a minimally paid, envelope-stuffer clerical job, but the atmosphere was dramatic, to say the least. There was a man named Jim Peck, a white man who believed in integration. He was on the first freedom rides in Birmingham. He was at many demonstrations and continually getting beaten up very badly. The phone calls would come in from Alabama and elsewhere saying Jim was in the hospital or in jail. All the real danger getting transmitted to the CORE office in New York City. And there were a lot of marches and I probably went to every one.

"The march on Washington in 1963 when Martin Luther King made his 'I Have a Dream' speech was significant in a personal way. I remember listening to King and looking around me. It was wall to wall people, no longer were we a small group of protesters. A lot had happened to the civil rights movement and to me since the days of picketing Woolworths. It felt like an eternity but it hadn't been that long ago. And those words coming over the loudspeakers, 'I have a dream . . .' I remember thinking about idealism and reality. This was definitely a turning point, a special time."

By that time Dylan had written his first political songs, "Masters of War," "Blowin' in the Wind," "Hard Rain's A-Gonna Fall," and "Lonesome Death of Hattie Carroll." But in spite of her political activism in that period, Susan tends to downplay her own part in influencing Dylan. "It was the climate of the times," she says. "People were interested in what was going on, because it was a carry-through from Woody Guthrie and Pete Seeger. The concerns that were on my mind were inevitably passed to him, and if he were not interested, he wouldn't have been interested. He obviously was."

As time went by, Dylan got more and more possessive of Susan. "There was a period when I was part of his possessions," says Susan. "I don't think he wanted me to do anything separate from him. He wanted me to be completely one hundred percent a part of what he was. He was tied up with his own development, and it was just his world that became concentrated in just music. The assumption is that the female doesn't really do anything, and he didn't enjoy the idea of me being separate from him."

As a result, Susan was "letting go of my other interests. And I was very much insecure and not self-confident. But," she adds, "somewhere deep down I must have had an instinct to survive . . . to have an identity of my own, not just as 'Dylan's girl.' I took classes at the School of Visual Arts, worked in the theater, and also had a waitressing job during the day. I made new friends who knew nothing

about my life with Dylan. I tried to keep both lives separate but it was difficult and I was under a lot of pressure.

"It's funny," she continues. "Dylan did say to me once,
'Never let anybody take up your space.' Which I always
thought was the most profound thing he ever gave me, one
of the best things he ever gave me. Because in spite of what
I appear to be, then or now, every woman has the tendency to be sucked in by the life of the man she is with,
and in spite of everything that was going on, I believe he
was aware of that. With that statement I felt he was ac-
knowledging the conflict I was in; he saw my vulnerability
and my strength. It meant a lot to me then, and after all
these years I still think it's a goodie."

In 1962, Susan had the opportunity to sail to Italy with
her mother and new stepfather, a college professor who
"couldn't believe that this woman he was marrying had two
vagabond daughters." She agonized over whether to go. "I
remember asking everybody, 'What do you think? Should

I go or shouldn't I go?' " In the end she went. Once she was in sunny Italy, Susan knew she'd made the right decision. She began to think of New York as "this dark tunnel—dark clubs and bars and somber." Here, she was also able to get a fresh perspective on her relationship with Dylan. She began to see that it had become "too heavy-duty—very grown, and all these people were older and all this stuff was going on. 'Cause we were too serious—too much too soon. He was too young for that kind of thing, and he was pursuing his career, which he was also single-minded about." At that point in her life, Susan knew that she could not be exclusive. "Something was wrong with the whole environment. It was fun, we had good times, but it became too exclusive. That's when I felt that I didn't want to be a string on his guitar, because I wasn't ready to retire. I hadn't even started out yet. And I saw that period in Italy as . . . let loose to be young again. It was in a town called Perugia. It was relaxing and the sun was shining and I was discovering life again. It was wonderful to be thrown into this, once I got over the terrible sadness of leaving my love at home."

Dylan, on the other hand, couldn't seem to stop missing her. "He would call me every day. He called and wrote, and I remember there was a turning point when he called and I didn't want to go to the phone. 'Cause I was enjoying life, which I should have been doing at eighteen."

In Italy, Susan met lots of new people, including the man who would become her husband some years later. But at the time, Susan stopped herself from getting totally involved with him because "I did want to resolve that relationship with Dylan."

So she returned to New York nearly a year later, feeling that she had grown up and matured in Italy and ready to handle anything that came her way. Dylan was still on tour in England when she got back, but his friends gave Susan quite a reception—although not the one she would have expected. "I was hit by all this gossipy stuff, with people saying, 'How could you leave him? How could you do that?' Coming back, apparently he had gotten even more famous. Certainly by writing to each other, he didn't write about his fame and fortune and all the bullshit that was going on. He was public property by then. When I came back from Italy, I was surrounded by these people I didn't even know intruding into my personal life. There were people who were actually angry that I had abandoned him at the 'most important time of his life.' I was 'the woman who deserted him.' "

One of the people, it seems, who was angry about Susan "deserting" Dylan was Johnny Cash. Susan, who had always been a fan of his, spotted him one night at the Gaslight and told the owner of the club that she would like to meet him. "And I remember the guy said, 'He'll probably want to meet you but not the way you want to meet him.' And I said, 'What do you mean?' He said, 'Well, because Johnny Cash had been with some woman who destroyed his life and he had a growing friendship with Dylan and he probably felt, 'Who's this bitch?' I thought, 'I'm someone Johnny Cash doesn't like. Oh, shit.' " When Susan was introduced to him, he "just kind of stonily looked at me. And I just said, 'You know, I really like your music,' and I said who I was, and he just nodded. But he didn't say, 'Sit down.' "

At another time, at another club, Susan remembers, "Somebody got up and sang, 'Don't Think Twice, It's All Right' with such vehemence, turning the song inside out, trying to tell me something, and then somebody else, to make me feel real weepy, sang, 'Tomorrow Is a Long Time.' *Everybody* was trying to be his spokesperson."

But someone must have spread the stories in the first place about Susan—and obviously, it was Dylan. "It's all his fault!" laughs Susan. "He mooned in public. He created the image of himself as the abandoned, wounded lover. I'm sure he was having a fine time also. Classic."

Even though Susan felt the attacks on her were unjustified ("I was not his wife or his property"), nevertheless she was shaken by people's responses to her. And by the time Dylan got back from London, Susan "was totally confused again. All my confidence had blown out the window."

Reunited with Dylan, Susan began to notice that there were some definite changes, and not for the better, in her boyfriend and his life-style. "There were a lot of people around him that I didn't like at all. It wasn't the old folksy crowd. He had bodyguards and managers. Just as Dylan got more and more famous, things got more and more oppressive and more and more people around him—bloodsuckers. I was more aware of ambition and infighting than I had been before."

All this depressed Susan. "It was all looking very bleak," she says. "It was a whole bad time, and I really crumbled. I had kind of a nervous breakdown. I began to see everyone as wanting my friendship and companionship just to get close to Bob. And that means everybody. And I also felt completely lost and confused and betrayed and I no longer knew who I could trust. And that included my sister, mother, Bob, everybody. It was devastating. And all I wanted to do was get away from it all and to recapture what Italy was for me. I knew that I wanted to live my own life and I really wanted to draw more than ever. And losing Bob to his fame and realizing that this is something beyond anything that I could conceive of being part of anymore. I didn't see myself as Bob Dylan's wife. Suddenly I saw it was something far away, knowing that I don't belong there for some reason, the way his life was."

So Susan began to wean herself away from Dylan, although they still kept in touch over the phone and occasionally saw each other. "I went to his concert in Forest Hills [in 1965] when the first part of the concert was acoustic and the second part was electric." Although Dylan was booed by some diehard folk fans during the second half,

Susan, for her part, loved it. "I guess they felt he was the
spokesman for these things and he betrayed them. But the
music goes on. You can't stay in one spot. I don't know
whether I told him that," Susan says softly, "because at
that time I was trying to be separate. But I liked what he
did. I remember talking to him afterward and I wonder if
I was as complimentary as I felt. But I hope so in retrospect, 'cause I really did feel that I did know him then,
that I did know what his music was."

How does Susan feel now about being the inspiration
for so many of Dylan's songs? She replies, "I got a really
touching phone call from Pete Seeger once, asking the same
question. It's just me and it was part of my life and I had
no idea it was this big, important influence. So to think
that I had an influence on him for songs, well, he had an
influence on me in my life. It's very nice to know if I'm in
the songs that are lovely, that I was an inspiration for them.
People have asked how I felt about those songs that were
bitter, like 'Ballad in Plain D,' since I inspired some of those,
too, yet I never felt hurt by them. I understood what he
was doing. It was the end of something and we both were
hurt and bitter. (If I could have written a song . . .) His
art was his outlet, his exorcism. It was healthy. That was
the way he wrote out his life . . . the loving songs, the
cynical songs, the political songs . . . they are all part of
the way he saw his world and lived his life, period. It was
a synthesis of feeling and vision and he made poetry from
it. He was like a sponge, he dove in very deep, absorbed
all he could, and then let it all out in his own unique way."

How did Susan feel when Dylan married Sara Lowndes
in 1965?

"Well, I knew Sara," she answers. "She was a friend of
Albert Grossman's wife, Sally, so we were friendly, all of
us. I just knew she was a Scorpio and she was in for it.
I'm a Scorpio, and he's a Gemini, and they don't mix."

A few years after the breakup with Dylan, Susan married the man she had met when she was in Italy. They lived in Italy for a while, where, as is the custom there, Susan kept her own maiden name. "But as soon as we were going to move to New York in 1970, I was right away going to cancel Rotolo off everything, because if my name was listed in the phone book, people were going to call, because they used to call all the time. They'd call to find out where he was. There were a lot of weirdos. He attracts weird fans. Poor guy. I don't know how he survived. I just didn't want any more. I wanted to live my own life. I didn't want to be this thing that was looked upon as something that was one step closer to God. 'Can you tell me what God is like?' and 'How did you like living with God?' It was Woodstock, and people were still praying to the great Allah, Dylan. I hated it. I felt pushed into a Bob Dylan identity that I didn't want to be. My identity for those years was no longer mine."

Susan and Dylan did not keep in touch. Then sometime in the mid-seventies, out of the blue he called. "He was with Lillian and Mell Bailey, old friends of both Bob and me. As I remember it, Mell was annoyed with Bob for calling me up again. 'Leave her alone, she's married.' I felt nervous, he wanted to see me, and I would have liked to see him but I was uncomfortable for my husband's sake. And I am sorry in a way. Screw it! Why didn't I see the guy? After all those years it would have been interesting. I shouldn't have gotten myself in the bind of protecting my husband's feelings over my own. That is why I value that statement, 'Never let anyone take up your space.'"

Claudette Robinson

SMOKEY ROBINSON

"By 1964, I'd had five miscarriages. At that time Smokey said, and Berry Gordy also, 'I think it's time for Claudette to come off the road.' "

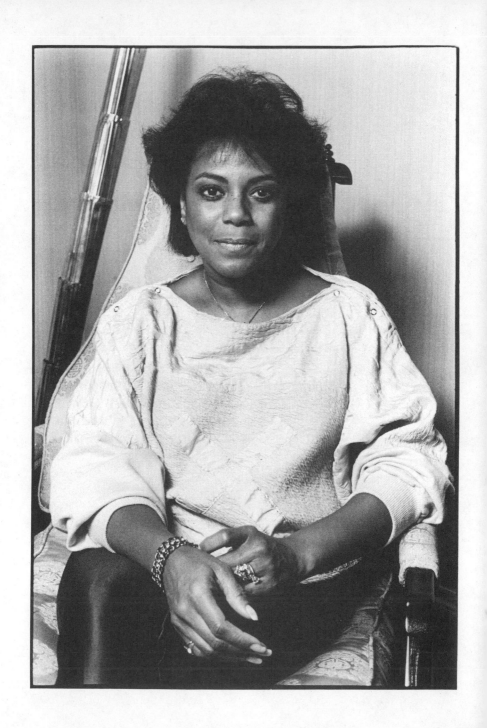

*M*otown singer and songwriter Smokey Robinson
and his wife, Claudette, go way back together: They have
known each other since they were children, hanging out
and singing on the same street corners together in a poor
neighborhood in Detroit. As a teenager, Claudette sang with
a girls' group, the Matadorettes, while Smokey headed up
the Matadors, the brother doo-wop group that included in
its members Claudette's brother, Emerson. When Emerson quit the group to join the army in 1957, Smokey, who
was dating Claudette, talked her into replacing her brother.
When Claudette joined, she never thought that the group
would ever be anything more than just a hobby. "In the
beginning I felt that we'd never make it in show business,"
recalls Claudette. "Black artists had such a difficult time
trying to get even heard on the radio, and these were the
ones who had been around a long time—Billy Eckstine and
Lena Horne and Sammy Davis. You could hear them on
the black stations but never what was considered the pop
stations. And I figured that basically, we were little kids."
At that time, Claudette was attending Wayne State College and planning to become a high school commerce
teacher.

By 1957, the Matadors had changed their name to the
Miracles and felt they were far along enough musically to
audition for singer Jackie Wilson's manager. In attendance
at their audition was a young songwriter by the name of
Berry Gordy, Jr. "Berry was very, very impressed with
the songs that we sang, and he wanted to know where we'd
gotten them, and Smokey said, 'I wrote them,' " Claudette

recalls. "Smokey had this one little spiral notebook with about a hundred songs, and he showed them to Berry."

At Gordy's urging, the Miracles recorded "Got a Job" in 1958, which succeeded in attracting some local attention. In 1959, just before the Miracles left on their first tour, Smokey and Claudette were married. "If we were going to be traveling on the road, in my day and time, people didn't start shacking up," says Claudette. "You were either married or your mother was with you."

In 1960 "Shop Around" became the first gold record for Smokey, Claudette, and the Miracles. In the years that followed, the group received a number of gold records for songs such as "I Second That Emotion" and "Tears of a Clown" and, all told, sold more than 60 million records and helped make Berry Gordy's Motown into the biggest black-owned corporation in the world. Along with Motown, the Robinsons relocated from Detroit to Los Angeles in 1972, where they live with their two teenage children—son, Berry, and daughter, Tamla, and Smokey's dad, Bill Robinson, Sr.

■ ■ ■

On one of the few streets in Beverly Hills where one can actually see children outside playing, the Robinson house looks like just about all the others—sturdy and expensive, but not flashy. Inside, it's large, roomy, with a lot of polished wood floors and mirrors and, on this particular day in May—except for the sound of Smokey working his Pac Man machine—very quiet. Dressed in a baggy shirt, tight black pants, and ballet slippers, Claudette Robinson sits on a leather couch in her living room with her legs tucked up underneath her. She looks over at a shelf at a photograph of herself and a very youthful-looking Smokey cutting their wedding cake (a rare sight in a rock household) and says, "Smokey and I are celebrating our twenty-fifth anniversary on November seventh," in a carefully modulated voice, enunciating every word. "And we still love and respect each other."

Just a few days after that picture was taken in 1959, Claudette, Smokey, and the three other Miracles left Detroit for their very first tour, which lasted five weeks and took them to New York and the Apollo Theater, Philadelphia, Baltimore, and Washington. As Claudette tells it, the road in those days was a lot different than it is today. "Today, when people have to do two shows, they cry. In some theaters, we did as many as eight shows in one day, and we were not even the only ones on the show. An example of one show we appeared on was the Supremes, Marvelettes, Marvin Gaye, Stevie Wonder, Temptations, Mary Wells, Contours. The show started at nine-thirty in the morning and sometimes, depending on where you were working, there were very few people out there." Claudette describes the Miracles in those early days as "just five kids learning what the business was about and meeting people that you'd read about in the newspapers but never thought you'd come into contact with. I'll always remember how helpful Jerry Butler was in telling us how we should stand on stage and how we should do our hands. 'Never let your palms out. Always keep them turned in. It has a more graceful look.' And he was absolutely correct."

On the road, the Miracles were not big drinkers or rowdy partiers, and the "guys" (as Claudette always refers to the other Miracles) always went out of their way to protect "little" Claudette from the seamy side of things. But there were some things that she couldn't help seeing—like all of the drug addicts around the Apollo Theater or, on another occasion, a "little girl who came up and asked one of the guys—not one of our guys—if he wanted to go to bed with her. She was eight years old." The thing that has stayed with Claudette most was the fact that girls were swarming backstage to see Smokey and the guys. "They didn't know that Smokey was my husband," she says. "Most people

Claudette and Smokey Robinson at home.

thought I was his sister. I remember this one girl was sitting across from us talking, and she had her legs like this. [Claudette spreads her legs wide.] She had no underwear on. I just couldn't believe it."

After the shows, the Miracles were supposed to attend question-and-answer sessions for their fans. What often ended up happening was that Smokey and the guys would just get up and leave in the middle of the session to go take a nap, leaving Claudette to fend with the fans by herself. Looking back, Claudette doesn't see that there was anything so terribly wrong with what the guys did. "By being the only female, I felt that I was going to have to work at it a little harder. To get people to know me and like me, I needed to spend more time than they did because they were guys and there were more females in the audience and they liked them because they were guys."

As the Miracles became more well known, they were spending more and more time on the road. It got to the point where they were touring about nine months out of every year in the early sixties. According to Claudette, this bothered Smokey a lot—"He's really a homeperson." But she didn't mind the traveling at all. "I felt I had my home with me because Smokey *was* my home." However, it was Claudette and not Smokey who was forced to stop touring on account of health problems. She was underweight and anemic. Worst of all, however, was the fact that Claudette suffered a series of miscarriages on the road. "By 1964, I'd had five miscarriages. At that time Smokey said, and Berry Gordy also, 'I think it's time for Claudette to come off the road.' " But Claudette didn't want to. "Each time I kept having those miscarriages my feeling was, 'I'll probably never have a baby, so why should I come off the road?' "

In the beginning, it was heartbreaking for Claudette to be left behind. "I would take them to the airport and cry. We had been together so much, not just Smokey and I but the other three guys as well. We were like a life, and when the other guys got married, their wives and their children, it became like a whole big family."

Claudette, however, found some consolation in the fact that she was permitted to record with the Miracles until Smokey's own departure from the group in 1972.

When Berry Robinson was born, much to Smokey and Claudette's joy, in 1968, Smokey cut back from touring in order to be with his family more. In 1972 he left the Miracles to take on more responsibilities in his position as a Motown vice-president. That lasted until 1974, when, at Claudette's urging, Smokey went back on the road. "He was missing something for himself. He wanted to stay at home with us but he missed that performing live onstage. It was so much a part of him and brought him a tremendous amount of joy, and for me to say, 'You can't go on the road again,' would have been just too unfair to him. To deprive his public of his talent would not be good, and I think he's been happier ever since. I don't think he would have done it on his own, because his loyalties are to the family."

Is Smokey faithful to Claudette when he's on the road? "As far as I know," chuckles Claudette. She goes on to say, "I don't think you can concentrate on what a person may or may not do in life, because as people become adults, they're probably going to do what they want to. And I think you have to have some sort of trust that they will do the right thing or be respectful of you in your marriage or relationship. And that's about as far as you can go, because to sit there and say, 'They will never ever do this,' same as parents say to their children, 'I know my kids will never do that.' You don't know. You just hope and pray."

Even when he's home, Smokey tends to have crazy hours—"sometimes his hours don't even start until he's going into the studio at eight, ten o'clock at night and not getting back until four, five o'clock in the morning"—so what

Claudette has tried to do over the years is be the balance
for the family. "If he has to be away from home, then I
always try to be here with the children. I let them know
they have some kind of security in terms of somebody's
going to be there—not a housekeeper."

In their spare time, Smokey and Claudette like to have
Pac Man competitions and go to the movies. On his own,
Smokey spends a lot of time on the golf course (Claudette
doesn't play). Knowing how much he likes it, she doesn't
try to take those times away from him unless she feels "he's
going too much."

Since the Matador days, Smokey has become much more
successful than Claudette ever dreamed possible. Claudette calls his success a "gift from God. I can recall in those
early years I thought Smokey was being much too extrav-
agant on gifts for me because he bought me minks and sa-
bles and chinchillas. I think, 'Here I am, still a young person
and I have shared in the material things of life that people
probably never would get a chance to. And I'm very happy
that I recognize that it's a gift from God and it's not anything that we did or anything else, because Smokey's talent is definitely a gift from God. A lot of people record
and nothing ever happens. So if you do make it in whatever you're gonna do, what a wonderful blessing that has
to be. You just have to continually give thanks to God for
all the great things that happen to you. People come and
go—their minds change, but that one stability of having
Christ's verses is the thing that keeps me going."

Now that her children are teenagers (and, it seems, typical
ones at that: Smokey is overheard grumbling about son
Berry's Grace Jones–style haircut), Claudette has decided
to take a stab at a singing career again—but this time around
as a soloist. For the last several months, she has been
working at putting an album together. Although Smokey
will not be producing it, he has given her his full support
and is contributing a couple of songs. The name of Clau-

dette's album will be *Identity*, and on the jacket only her first name will appear. "There will not be a Robinson," she says. "Yes, I am Smokey Robinson's wife, but I also have a name, the name I had long before I knew him. I would like to be identified with that name."

inda Lawrence Leitch

BRIAN JONES;
DONOVAN LEITCH

"There was tons of fan mail pouring in and Brian sitting there and reading it and saying, 'Did Mick get more than me this week?' "

*I*n 1962, fifteen-year-old British schoolgirl Linda Lawrence was one of ten people who showed up at a small jazz club in Windsor, England, to hear a new rhythm and blues band called the Rolling Stones. Although Linda didn't know the first thing about rhythm and blues—she was more of a jazz fan—she ended up dancing to the Stones' music all night. After the show, she told Rolling Stone Brian Jones how much she liked his music. As it turned out, Brian and Linda ended up going out for two years; the relationship ended after Linda bore him a son, Julian, out of wedlock in 1964.

Unhappy as Linda was about the breakup, through Brian she had met and made friends with many of the pivotal people in the swinging London social and music scene in the mid-sixties. One of these people was Donovan Leitch, one of the quintessential singer/songwriters of the sixties British invasion, who brought us songs like the folky "Catch the Wind," the psychedelic "Mellow Yellow," and the flower-power "Hurdy-Gurdy Man." Linda and Donovan were married in 1970.

In the years that followed, Donovan pretty much disappeared from the charts. During that period the Leitches lived a quiet life in the California desert, raising Julian (whom Donovan adopted) and their own two daughters, Astrella and Oriole. Today they divide their time between Windsor, England, and California.

. . .

In the ever-increasing number of biographies on the Rolling Stones, Linda Lawrence is usually portrayed as a very determined, persistent young woman, who, after being jilted by Brian Jones, refused to give up hope that one day he would become a responsible father to Julian.

With only this to go by, one would think that in person Linda would come across as loud and aggressive. This is not the case. Linda Leitch sits curled up on a couch in her rather mystical-looking living room decorated with Indian prints, sipping at her rose hips tea laced with honey; speaks in soft, whispery, at times barely audible tones; and is willowy-thin, almost to the point of frailty. And in her eyes there is a little wistful look. Still, one can detect from the way that Linda tells her story—which sounds like something out of a picaresque novel—a strong will and determination; once she begins to talk, she stays firmly on track and seems to get so deeply involved in getting her story told that at times she is oblivious to questions and other distractions.

With the exception of a few years in Canada, Linda Lawrence grew up in the town of Windsor, outside London. When Linda was a teenager in the early sixties, Windsor had a little informal club over the top of a pub that served as a jazz club. "I was into jazz," says Linda. "I was what they called a beatnik and I hated pop and Cliff Richard and all that." In any event, one evening when Linda was about fifteen and on the verge of leaving school, the usual jazz group didn't turn up, and it was announced that in its place a rhythm and blues group would play. "I didn't know what that meant," says Linda. "But I was curious and went along. And it was the Stones, and there were only about ten people there, so . . . the music was amazing. A couple of girls and I, we just danced all night and had a fantastic time. After the show, we met them, obviously because there was only the Stones and the ten of us. Like boys and girls at that age, they said, 'Would you like a drink at the bar?' " Linda, who remembers being "terribly turned on" by Brian's harmonica and slide-guitar-playing, found herself talking to Brian straight away. In the course of the conversation, he mentioned that the Stones would be playing at a place called Ken Colyer's in London the next day. "Brian asked me to come along and I did. Every time they were playing somewhere, I would go. But again, at Ken Colyer there were only about twenty people. They didn't all of a sudden make it." With every club date, however, the number of people in attendance grew, as did the relationship between Brian and Linda. She says, "After we'd been going out with each other for a few months, my parents wanted to meet Brian, so he put on a nice clean shirt and brought them up to Richmond. After that, Brian came down to dinner a few times and loved the family so much that he kind of moved in 'cause his flat wasn't very nice."

At that time, Mick, Keith, and Brian shared a shabby two-room flat in Edith Grove, Chelsea. "It was Brian's flat to begin with. He had one room to himself, and Keith and Mick would share the other one. They were all sort of still living at home, but this is where they had a kind of flat, their own independence. No food, and the kitchen was filthy, and these typical boys all living together." There was no telephone in the flat either, though "there was a phone box at the end of the road, and I do remember Brian always getting up and running down there, calling people like Eric Easton (a London agent). I'm not sure how he made that connection, but when he did, it was to the Regency Street office, and Brian would be the one who'd dress up smart and go down and see him." Brian, as the story goes, always felt that he should be paid higher wages than the other four Stones. Quite true, says Linda. "Because he felt he did more work. Which he did. He was very money-conscious, but Pisces seem to be [Linda, who is a firm believer in the ways of astrology, frequently makes references to things like "charts" and "signs" in her conversation].

"Besides money he wanted control of the music direction," she continues. "He had control right up until Andrew [Loog Oldham, the Stones' first manager] came on the scene." Linda remembers *that* day quite clearly. "It was in Redding or somewhere, and I remember Andrew coming down to the gig and telling everybody what they should be doing, and all of a sudden there was this other person. They had to change their image and ideas, and because Brian was so strong-minded himself, he clashed with Andrew immediately. Had they taken a bit more time with each other, they might have got on very well. But being very young and both having their ideas, Brian instinctively and intuitively must have felt, 'Uh-oh.' In his mind he'd lost some power and control. Up until then I felt he felt quite confident that he was taking the music where he wanted to take it."

At that point in time, none of the Stones were writing their own songs, but Linda can remember Brian sitting off by himself in a room in her parents' house composing songs and "fiddling with the guitar—in a very insecure way, never wanting to play it to anyone else or let anyone else hear it. Which was strange—it would be just getting his own personal thoughts down."

Contrary to stories that Brian would physically and verbally abuse his girlfriends, Linda says that Brian was every inch the gentleman. "I found him a very soft, gentle, polite person. He'd treat a lady like a lady. I like that. I can open my own doors, but I like someone to try to open first. Mick and Keith were more rowdy and they were younger by a couple of years, so they had a different kind of attitude. I just found that Brian was the more mature one. I just thought Mick was quite funny—his thing on stage and his singing."

By this time, Linda had quit school and was commuting to London from Windsor every day to attend the Morris School of Hairdressing in Piccadilly. Some nights she'd stay with her aunt in the city so that she'd have the chance to see the Stones, who were playing more frequently in London proper and whose audiences seemed to be getting bigger by the minute. Meanwhile, the Stones' Liverpudlian rivals, the Beatles, had already made it to the top of the charts in England. Linda remembers that on a couple of occasions, they came down to Richmond to check out the Stones. What was Linda's impression of the Fab Four? She replies with a laugh, "Because I was with the Stones, I didn't like the Beatles." Of the four, though, John Lennon was the one who stands out in her memory. "He always seemed so sarcastic. But at least he made you think every time he said something, rather than a boring statement. He'd say something like, 'There's a cat in the cupboard over there.' I'd go to the cupboard, and of course there wasn't. I remember thinking, 'Now, why did he say that?' "

By now, Brian had officially moved into Linda's parents' house. "He was doing his washing, borrowing my brother's shirts . . ." Didn't Linda's parents object to his having moved in? "Oh, no. They loved him. They lent him our car and everything. The Rolling Stones didn't have any transport. They had one van, which was Stew's [Ian Stewart, an early member of the Rolling Stones who was eventually kicked out by their manager for looking too normal] and they'd all pile in, and Brian always liked his own thing—to be a little bit separate. My dad used to let him use our car, which was a Vauxhall. It was quite a nice car, and he was always bumping it coming back from a gig. He was tired and full of beer and a stop sign and a car in front and Brian would just . . . not major accidents, just little bumps."

In Linda's opinion, Brian took to her family in the way he did because they were so different from his own family. "He had real straight parents—very different from my family 'cause we were all open and everything was always happening there." One day Brian drove Linda down to Cheltenham to meet his parents, in her dad's car, of course.

"We were almost at his house, a few blocks away, and he got a terrible attack of asthma—Brian had asthma—I was always carrying his 'squirter'—and I realized that he was getting very emotional about going back to see his parents. Anyway, we went and stayed a couple of days. I was put in the daughter's bedroom, and Brian slept on the couch downstairs. Dinnertime was a certain time—very traditional kind of attitude."

In the course of their visit, Brian's parents were showing Linda some pictures, when it slipped out that Brian had made a girl pregnant when he was fifteen. Linda remembers that they were "still kind of upset with Brian" over that, primarily because he'd had to leave school—though the disclosure didn't bother her, particularly. "I didn't have prejudices and I wasn't brought up to think that somebody was wrong for doing something that might have been a mistake."

Brian's parents, says Linda, were also kind of unhappy about their son being in a rock and roll band. "They didn't like it at all. My first reaction was that I didn't feel that they were very proud of him, but he wanted them to be. That went on every time we went down. But as he got more and more famous, they seemed to get more and more friendly, and he tried hard. I remember him sending telegrams when he got busted. I'd always wonder why did he bother, but of course you do. You want recognition from the people closest to you."

Linda and Brian had been seeing each other for about a year when she got pregnant. She herself was not too upset by the discovery because, she says, "We were going to get married and we were looking at houses and everything felt okay." Although Linda's parents were upset, they were, as always, very supportive. But it was a different story with Brian's parents. Linda and her parents had gone down to Cheltenham to try breaking the news to them. "We took them out for a drink in the pub and we were all sitting there and we just couldn't get it out. We thought if we'd take them for a drink, they'd relax, but they didn't. So my parents wrote a letter about what was going on. And they were very nasty and sent this awful letter back, which I have to this day, saying 'That's impossible. We don't see how it could have happened.' "

In the beginning of her pregnancy, Brian treated Linda well. But as time went on, he became less and less interested in her. The change in attitude came, Linda feels, sometime during the Stones' first American tour in June 1964. "I got cards and letters from him saying he loved me. Then Brian took all these strange psychedelic drugs. When he came back, he was like a different person. And Andrew and everyone was saying, 'Oh, the publicity. If you get married, your career will be finished,' and all of a sudden Brian felt they were saying, 'Oh, family man,' making Brian feel very insecure. He already was, and it didn't help." Because of Brian's change of attitude, Linda, accompanied by Brian; Mick's girlfriend, Chrissie Shrimpton; and Charlie Watts's wife, Shirley, went to a doctor to investigate the possibility of having an abortion.

"I went in, and all they asked me was, 'Do you love this boy?' and I said yes, and then they asked Brian the same thing, and they said they wouldn't do it because we could make something of it if we wanted to." So Linda went through with the pregnancy, though she remembers that Brian kept trying to hide her. "But I was so insistent and wanted to go everywhere still." Apparently, Linda's presence on the road with the Stones used to cause some arguments, because "right from the beginning they didn't like girls going with them because they wanted to meet other girls. But," says Linda with a smile, "they couldn't quite say I couldn't, because Brian used my dad's car. But Chrissie used to get mad and say, 'Well, Linda's going,' and I'd always start off all these arguments. We [Linda and Chrissie] were always comforting each other."

Brian and Linda's son, Julian, was born in July 1964. By that time the Stones were quite famous. "There was tons of fan mail pouring in and Brian sitting there and reading it and saying, 'Did Mick get more than me this week?' He did manage to get more mail than Mick most of the time." Linda's mother still has many of the fan letters packed away in boxes in her house. Someday Linda means to put them in a book for Julian. "There's some wonderful things in there—all the things that Brian looked for; the support, and he just wanted to be loved by as many people as he could possibly have. 'Cause he had such a tight, unloving upbringing. Mick had much more of an ego than Brian. Brian had no confidence, and it was more of a fight for love and recognition of how great a talent he was."

A few months after the birth of Julian, the Stones took off for their second U.S. tour ("when Brian left for America, he was telling me how to feed Julian 'cause he'd had a child!"), and that trip was what in Linda's mind really finished off the relationship. On the tour, Brian was the butt of still more teasing about being a dad. "And then when he came back, it was 'Oh, I can't get married.' He took everything away from my parents' and got his own place. He had money now. He came back and bought my parents a handbag and a wall clock and he felt very emotional toward them, as if he wanted to let them know that he did appreciate all the time they'd given him."

In her heart, Linda knows that Brian "really felt he was being rotten to me and cutting me up but that he was trying to say to me, 'You're too good for me, so I don't want to drag you through all this, but I must go and I have to do this.' And he was trying to make me feel not too bad about the fact that he was going to leave, because he took me on a trip to Morocco." For Linda, the trip to Morocco was quite an eye-opener. "It was as if he was trying to make me independent and have an experience, which he certainly did. I'd never been anywhere other than Canada. This is where I met his first hangers-on." A popular Parisian model was one of the characters in Brian's entourage. She took Linda along on some of her modeling shoots to "these wonderful palaces. We dressed up in caftans and had pictures taken. And then she started getting very close to me, and I realized she was bisexual. I was very upset, 'cause I was in love with Brian and I thought he was bringing me to get closer instead of . . . And of course they were smoking and getting high, and I had never done drugs before. The cakes and cookies and the mint tea had hash in it."

Brian ended the relationship when they returned to England. "They had tours booked and they were off around the world, and Brian had said that he probably wouldn't see me again." Linda was devastated, though fortunately friends dragged her out to parties in an attempt to get her out of her depression. At one party, given by London art dealer and friend to the rock stars Robert Fraser, Linda was given LSD for the first time. "They put something in the drink and they put on this great African music, and I thought I was drunk. Apparently I was dancing—I picked up maracas and bongos. I probably thought I was in Africa or something. And they all danced with me."

At another party for a popular music television program called *Ready Steady Go!* she met Donovan, who was at that time a regular on the show but had not yet made any records. "With Don, it was in an instant, just like it was with Brian. Just eye contact. No words. And he came over and asked me if I would dance. And we danced amazingly well together."

Right from the start, Linda felt close to Don. "In some ways Don and Brian were amazingly alike—although Don's a Taurus and Brian's a Pisces. They were both gentlemen to me, very polite and considered my parents and wanted to meet them. But Don's whole thing after the Stones had built up to be so crazy was so gentle and so warming."

**Linda Leitch with daughters,
Astrella and Oriole.**

But when a few months later Don asked Linda to marry him (Linda later discovered that he had gone out and bought a lace wedding dress for her in Portobello Road), she refused. "My reaction was, 'Oh, no, I don't want another relationship. I'll get myself together and get independent.' " And Linda had some business to take care of, too: She was determined to go to America to try and discover just what had happened to Brian to have made him change so much.

The opportunity to find out presented itself in the form of a very rich young American boy named Allan. "I'd gone to the Scotch Club—I was always there with Brian—and somebody came up to me and tapped me on the shoulder and said, 'Oh, you belong on a surfboard. I can get you a job in America and you can be a model.' And it was this Allan. He was the groupie of the pop stars. He knew everybody, and everybody knew him. When the Stones and the Beatles first went to America, it was Allan that was throwing all the parties and gave them all the drugs and set everything up. Everyone loved Allan, but he was a bit of a cold soul that you felt sorry for him, even though he was the one with all the money. At the Scotch Club, he had a girlfriend with him, so he wasn't trying to chat me up. So he seemed genuinely interested in helping me. So I got the money together, and he took me to the U.S. embassy and helped me fill in the forms and helped me get my visa."

It was Allan who set Linda up with places to stay when in 1965 she made the first of what would be several trips to the United States. After depositing Julian with her parents (who thought Linda should have the chance to see the world), Linda flew to New York and worked as a nanny for Mary Travers (of Peter, Paul, and Mary) and her husband, photographer Barry Feinstein. "They were in the middle of arguing and having a split-up, so after a week or so I went on to Los Angeles."

In L.A., Allan arranged for her to stay with an actress

who appeared in all of the bikini beach films. "I watched this crazy girl with this blond hair dressed in bikinis, and it was funny listening to her say her parts. I thought I'd met a movie star! And Lenny Bruce was living above us. He always seemed to be just sitting around listening to everybody." To make money, Linda did odd jobs—doing people's hair, making clothes, or helping out with children. But it wasn't enough to live on, so she cashed in her return ticket to London and got an apartment on Sunset Strip—she knew about the street from the television show— conveniently situated within easy walking distance of her two favorite clubs, the Whiskey and the Trip. It was at one of these clubs that Linda met a girl with whom she is still friends today, a fourteen-year-old high school sophomore named Cathy Cozy (who would some years later marry John Sebastian of the Lovin' Spoonful). Cathy and her friends were all Stones fans and were very impressed that Linda had been Brian's girlfriend. They also liked Linda's wardrobe, which included several items such as tailored suits from Brian's own closet. "All these girls came up from Long Beach and would borrow my clothes. And if I wasn't in my apartment, they'd turn up at the club dressed in my clothes."

After a time, Linda ran out of money again, so her young friend Cathy Cozy's family let her stay with them, but only on the condition that Linda attend Fairfax High School with Cathy every day. "It was fun," says Linda. "It was really different from English schools because you seemed to be able to skip lessons. I liked the sewing classes. But then we both got bored and fed up with it, and I said I had to go back to England to see my parents and Julian." And by this time she was ready to see Donovan again. "But by the time I got round to it and went back to Don in England, he'd met this American girl, Enid, just after I'd let him down. Enid was one of those girls that you get introduced to at the end of a gig and she's in the limousine." Linda knew all about those kind of girls, because whenever she and Cathy were in a club, they used to get hit on by these women, who would ask if they wanted to meet some of the groups in town. "These girls would say, 'Come down and you'll make some money. You don't have to sleep with them but just hang out with them.' But of course they all did. So Don was introduced to one of these girls, and I'd heard this and I thought, 'Oh, God, no.' Because immediately they got in the car, they don't talk or anything and they'd take their top off. And she got Don hooked because he was heartbroken." Enid, as it turned out, got pregnant by Don. When Linda heard that, she thought she'd really lost her chance at getting him back. "But as I listened to his songs, I would feel that he was talking to me and I got more hope and I'd say to Cathy, 'You know, he doesn't love her because he would have married her by now.' So I kept hoping."

Whenever Linda was in England, she'd always make a point of finding out where Brian Jones was and take Julian round to see him. "One time I took him to see Brian, Brian was in Richmond Hospital with kidney trouble. It was very strange for both of them because of not seeing each other. That was the last time I saw Brian before he died."

Linda heard about Brian's death when she was in California. "I was asleep and I got a phone call from Michael Aldrid, who was the announcer on the *Ready Steady Go!* program. I just went crazy. I always thought we'd get together and have a chat. I kept waiting and thinking, 'Eventually he'll come round.' It was mostly for Julian to keep in touch with Brian. I immediately got a ticket together— Phil Spector lent me the money—and I flew straight home and went to the funeral. I took Julian with me and I was treated rather rudely by Bill Wyman's wife, who said, 'What are you doing here?' and I felt like saying, 'Well, what are you doing here?' Anyway, I went back to Brian's parents' house after the funeral, and they held Julian for a while, which I was pleased about."

On her last stay in California, Linda took a job as a

housekeeper for another twenty-one-year-old millionaire named Jonathan Debenham, who had made his money by inventing *The Dating Game*. "He was a vegetarian, and I could have my own room and bring Julian," says Linda. "He had just been to India and he meditated. He knew a lot about astrology. He was a Scorpio and he read my charts, and I read his. That's how we got to know each other. Jonathan had a different girl every night from *The Dating Game*, so I saw this whole thing going on that was very strange. But he totally had respect for me. I was living this nice, respectable life cooking vegetarian food. Jonathan had brought back this Indian friend with him, and he started teaching me how to make great meals out of potatoes and at the same time meditation. So when Donovan and the Beatles were in India, I was going on this parallel path with Don. But then all of a sudden, one day Jonathan just freaked out. He wanted to sell everything, give up everything, hated himself and who he was. He gave away

Photo by: Suzanne Tenner © 1985

his cars and said I didn't have this work anymore. It totally freaked me out. Julian and I had nowhere to go."

Then she met country-singer/songwriter Gram Parsons.
"I went to stay with Gram and began to think that I was
going to fall in love again. I seemed to get thrown back
into music and going back to clubs and I met the Byrds
and the Eagles and I learned about country rock music. But
then he met the Stones and started getting on heroin, so I
then retreated. But while this was happening, we were going
to the desert a lot to Joshua Tree, a whole bunch of us and
taking mushrooms. When we were out there, they were
making a film of the last Flying Saucer Convention. While
we were there, Julian started messing around with the fire
and running in front of the camera. But the director loved
him so much that he started using Julian as the center of
the story. Michelle Phillips was in it and other people, and
they were quite upset that Julian stole the show."

With Julian in the movies, money was at last coming in
regularly. Linda and Julian were put up at the Château
Marmont, and everything was going along just fine, when
all of a sudden the backer for the film cut off the funds.
"He was one of these totally crazy people who had German shepherds in his office, he was so paranoid. He found
out there was a scene with a dead Viet Nam guy in front
of a meat counter in the supermarket, and Julian was this
little boy all dressed up with this little bag that came from
another planet. It freaked him out. He thought it was too
political.

"After this was cut off," Linda continues, "I said, 'I'm
going to go back to England and buy a little cottage and
make clothes and sell them, and Julian and I will live in
the little cottage together, and I won't think of finding the
right man again.'"

As it happened, after Linda returned to England, she ran
into an old friend who offered her a space in a cottage in
Hertfordshire. Linda drove out to take a look at the place

and found, strangely enough, Donovan sitting on a bed upstairs! "It was his cottage and he was supposed to be on a world tour and he almost had a nervous breakdown and he was almost in tears."

Linda must have been what the doctor ordered, because Donovan rose from the bed, and the two of them walked out into the forest and sat in the fields. "He had his guitar and he just started playing. And this cow came up and gave us both a great lick! And he looked at me, and I looked at him, and we never left each other since. We got married in Windsor. We've been married thirteen years, but we've known each other twenty."

After they were married, Donovan adopted Julian. Today, Julian is a grown man of twenty-one, lives in his own van on their property in California, and, with his "huge head with very straight hair," looks, according to Linda, quite a bit like his father. "His whole life is music. He sings in this little club in a town in California and he has a bass guitar, which he plays a great riff on. Funnily enough, in his performance style he's just like Mick Jagger, which is very funny because Brian was always jealous of Mick's certain things, which Julian very unconsciously seems to have picked up. Julian's really into the Stones. When Julian was sixteen, Mick let him go on the road with them and took him in the jet, and Julian stood backstage and imitated everything Mick did, and Shirley says it freaked Mick out, because he thought this shadow was following him."

Julian has been given just about every book on his father. "Julian's always had total respect," says Linda. "I've never given him any reason to hate. But he's read everything about Brian, and there's been a lot of distorted pictures of Brian and his violence."

How have Linda and Donovan handled the ups and downs of Donovan's career in the last ten years or so? Linda answers, "We didn't even notice it. We were in the desert with the girls and we were in such bliss and into our thing. He constantly made records anyway."

These days Linda and Donovan have been working together on a pet project: a musical for the stage called *The Lives of the Wives*, which will be based on three women's attitudes and opinions of their lives with famous musicians from the sixties, the seventies, and the eighties. If the project does get off the ground, one of the things Linda hopes to accomplish with it is to enlighten the general public about the behavior of rock stars. Take all those stories about the rock stars who fool around on the road, for example. "That's in life everywhere," says Linda. "You could probably find that same thing with businessmen traveling with their secretaries. I don't like it that it's just the rock and rollers being blamed for decadence.

"I have lived more life than most do twice my age, and this play we write is a study of truly heroic feminism—woman's liberation aside—I liberated myself with no compromise—which isn't easy in the music world—but it's been worth it."

 *Marilyn Wilson*

BRIAN WILSON

*"I had girls in my own house
knocking on his bedroom door.
. . . I was known as the bitch wife."*

*O*ne night in Hollywood in 1962, fourteen-year-old Marilyn Rovell went to a music club called Pandora's Box to catch the performance of a local band called the Beach Boys. The group, composed of the Wilson brothers—Brian, Dennis, and Carl—their cousin Mike Love and friend Al Jardine, had just scored a local hit, "Surfin'," and another single, "Surfin' Safari," was climbing the national charts. Marilyn's cousin, Ginger Blake, was dating Gary Usher, a friend of the Beach Boys, and during the course of the evening he introduced Marilyn to Brian Wilson, the creative force behind the group. As it turned out, Marilyn and Brian had a lot in common: Marilyn herself came from a musical background and from time to time would perform around town with her sister, Diane Rovell, and cousin, Ginger Blake, as a backup "girl group." They called themselves the Honeys—the surfers' girls. That night, Brian told Marilyn that he was interested in recording the girls. But his interest in Marilyn was not just on the professional level, and vice versa. In 1964, Marilyn dropped out of high school to marry Brian. "I learned more from Brian at sixteen than I could have ever learned at any school," says Marilyn. "The man is brilliant. And I also loved looking at him." In the first years of his marriage, Brian Wilson wrote and produced some of his greatest music—"Good Vibrations" (1966) and the *Pet Sounds* album (1966). The Wilsons have two daughters—Carnie, born 1968, and Wendy, born 1969.

■　■　■

You'd think that the woman that Beach Boy Brian Wilson married at the peak of his career would look like those

California girls he idealized in his songs: leggy, tanned, and blond. But Marilyn Wilson is short, dark-haired, Jewish (and from Chicago, no less!), and when you get right down to it, looks as though she'd be more at home in Bloomingdale's than on the beach. "It's true—I can barely swim," giggles Marilyn. She sounds a little out of breath—and for good reason, it turns out. She is throwing a Sweet Sixteen party for her daughter Carnie the next day, and she's been dashing around trying to get her large mock Tudor house in Encino, California—complete with tennis court, swimming pool, and Jacuzzi—in order before all the guests, who will include Beach Boy Carl Wilson and his wife, Annie, arrive.

The house seems to be filling up with early arrivals; Marilyn's parents and some of their friends are hanging out at the kitchen table. And, wandering around the house, nibbling on Bit O' Honey candy bars, are Marilyn's singing partners: Ginger and Diane.

When Marilyn and the Honeys first met the Beach Boys, they used to get together to sing over at the Wilson brothers' house in the evenings. "Brian was fascinated by women to begin with," says Marilyn. "He just took a liking to us and liked the different sounds of our voices and he was kind of infatuated. And he said, 'Hey, I'd like to record you girls.' And Brian used to talk to his dad [who was also the Beach Boys' manager at the time] about us. His father liked the idea of Brian working with the girls—it was a good outlet.

"We all just got to be real good friends. Diane and Carl and David Marks and myself all went to the same school— Hollywood Professional School, because we all had music careers. And Carl and David would drive from Hawthorne and come pick Diane and me up, and we would all go to school together, and then they'd drive us home, usually have lunch at our house."

After Marilyn got married to Brian, she would go to all his recording sessions, "watching him from start to finish."

Even for a rock musician, Marilyn's husband was very, very obsessive about his music. "Brian's whole life was eating and at the piano," says Marilyn. "Every time he'd get a new line he'd wake me up out of bed, drag me out—'Hey, you gotta come listen to this!' My whole life was sitting there at the piano with him, and that"—Marilyn points to a piano that stands in the middle of her living room—"is the piano, for many, many albums, *Pet Sounds* . . ." She points to the needlepoint cover on the piano bench, emblazoned with the first few bars of "Surfer Girl." "I made that for him," she says. "We'd be watching TV, and I had it in a bag and I'd be sitting there stitching away, my fingers almost bleeding. For the three months it took to do that bench, he never asked me, 'What are you doin', Mar?' "

While Brian was carrying the load of the writing, arranging, and producing for most of the Beach Boys' albums in the sixties, he also found time to inspire, rehearse, and write songs for his wife's girl group, the Honeys—an unusually unselfish act for a rock husband with a career in full force. "What Brian taught us was style and how to make a record from start to finish," says Marilyn. "Brian was my number one fan. Brian always told me from day one, 'You have the greatest voice.' "

With Brian's help, the Honeys got a record deal with Capitol Records, who pushed them as a "Beach Girls" group. For promotional pictures, Marilyn, Diane, and Ginger wore bouffant hairdos and toted surfboards. Their single, "Surfin' Down the Swanee River"/"Shoot the Curl" was Brian's first major production effort outside the Beach Boys. It flopped commercially, as did a Honeys (briefly reborn as Spring) album, produced by Brian in 1971—although the latter was liked by critics. "Brian could never understand why we never had a hit record," says Marilyn. "He had more faith in us than anyone." Apparently, the rest of the Beach Boys did not. "The Beach Boys never supported the Honeys," says Marilyn darkly. "The rest of

**The Honeys: Marilyn Wilson with her cousin
Ginger Blake and sister Diane Rovell.**

the guys were jealous of Brian giving us any of Brian's time."

Ginger Blake, who has wandered into the living room, offers an explanation for their behavior: "There were a lot of family problems, he and his brothers."

And Brian, as it happened, had some severe personal problems of his own. In 1964, the year Brian and Marilyn were married, Brian was under enormous stress from classic rock star pressures of trying to stay on top of the charts, extending his musical range, and keeping up with the responsibilities of touring. During a two-week tour of Texas, he cracked. This was the beginning of his long slide into mental deterioration over the next few years (he would not go on the road again for another seven years). At first no one, not even Marilyn, was aware of the depth of Brian's problems. She says, "It's hard to notice it every day when you're living with someone. You don't see the little bit of down, down, down, down. You say, 'He'll be better in a couple of weeks or a month or so.' But he just kept getting worse. And to be honest, I never really got the support from the Beach Boys that there was anything wrong with Brian for a long time. They don't know what it was like behind the doors. Brian would tell me his deepest thoughts, his fears and problems. He was very paranoid. People were out to get him. People were gonna kill him. It was heart-breaking."

Marilyn, who had looked up to Brian as her mentor, found herself in a new role. "I had depended on Brian to make so many decisions," she says. "I had so much faith in him until he started losing it mentally. Then I became the parent."

As Brian got worse, Marilyn's work with the Honeys began to slide. "It just got so pushed aside because of my responsibilities—there was no one else to do what I had to do. I had to raise children and help run a Beach Boy organization. It got to the point where I was signing checks all the time for all the guys. They needed someone dependable. And there was so much going on with Brian that I didn't feel the pain of not being successful."

Brian had been in the habit of experimenting with a variety of drugs, and Marilyn is convinced that those had been the cause of his illness. "I know it was the damned drugs, the LSD, any mind-expanding drugs," she says. "There are some people who can take the same drugs and never get affected, but Brian is a supersensitive person." But with Brian's studio right in their own house, Marilyn discovered that it was impossible to keep drugs away from him. "I had twenty, thirty people in my house every day," she recalls. "I had girls in my own house knocking on his bedroom door. I didn't know who was who. And Brian would walk into a room and say, 'Hey! Anybody got anything?' And someone would be honored to give him something."

Finally Marilyn put her foot down and threw all the "leeches," as she calls them, out of her house. "It got to the point where I was getting older and I said, 'Now, wait a minute. I'm tired of people telling me how I live. This is my home. I'm raising children. I'm gonna say who comes in, who doesn't.' No one could stand me because I didn't want those people in my home. I was known as the bitch wife. And I was just a total bitch because I knew that they were giving him stuff and they were helping him be sicker." Marilyn sighs. "The money and success are wonderful, but they don't know what it's like to live with someone who's mentally disabled. They don't know what it's like to watch someone deteriorate."

Apparently the only thing that wasn't deteriorating about Brian was his music, although he was going to some odd lengths in order to compose his songs. "He had a carpenter come in and build a little wood wall around the whole dining room, and they came in and put eight tons of sand in the middle. The piano was sitting in the middle of the sand. He wanted to feel what it was like to have your feet in the sand and then write in it." Marilyn laughs uneasily. "It was strange, but what can I say? It worked."

By 1976 the strain of dealing with Brian's illness alone was too much for Marilyn. She says, "Brian started getting really bad when Carnie was around nine. I said, 'I do not want to bring these children up in a household where there's someone walking around who's very sick. You can't help a person who doesn't want to help himself, and Brian did not want to help himself—I don't think he knew how to. Most people face their problems, and it is painful because life is painful. Brian never really had to—he was a big star. You can say something horrible to someone, and people would laugh and go along with it just because of who you are. That's wrong, because you start to feel like the freak that people make you out to be.

"I finally had to go to a doctor because I felt like I was

Marilyn Wilson with her parents, Irving and Mae Rovell.

a rope, with the kids at one end and Brian at the other end. I knew I had to find a really special doctor who was as unique as Brian was with his music and mind. Also, Brian could con anybody into anything. I knew that he needed someone who wouldn't take his bullshit, who could call him on it."

The "really special" doctor turned out to be Dr. Eugene Landy, a controversial name in psychotherapy who had invented something called twenty-four-hour therapy. Instead of talk sessions, Landy's staff lived with Brian ("They want a total controlled environment") and taught him how to cope with the basics of daily living—like getting out of bed in the morning, fixing a meal, or driving a car. After a couple of years under Landy, Marilyn says, Brian "felt he was strong enough to say, 'I don't need you anymore.'" Also there was pressure on Brian from the Beach Boys' camp (especially from manager Mike Love, who didn't like Landy) to stop the treatment.

Like many people who live with a mentally ill person, Marilyn discovered that while she had been taking care of Brian, she had been neglecting to take care of herself. "When I was married, it was all Brian and Brian first. There wasn't that personal need for myself, which was one of my problems. I left myself out of myself. The thing that helped me was taking est. That's when I realized, 'Hey. There is Marilyn. What happened to Marilyn? Who's thinking about me?' I did everything for Brian and my kids, but I forgot about myself. The thing that est taught me was that you're not going to change anything. You have to do what makes you happy for you."

In 1979 Marilyn decided that she would be better off without Brian, and they split up. "It just got to the point where he really wasn't getting better with me there. I didn't want to deal with it anymore because I just couldn't. And, see, I wanted him to be a father to the children, and he didn't want to be. He couldn't be a father when he needed help himself." They were divorced in 1981.

These days, Marilyn is a single parent raising two teen-age girls. As for men, she hasn't met anybody very "honest or genuine. They go after me for my money." But she's not sitting around at home waiting for Prince Charming: She recently went back to school and got her high school diploma. And Marilyn, Ginger, and Diane recently got back together again as the Honeys, and this time around they're taking themselves very seriously. "The real need to become famous was after my divorce," says Marilyn. They've made a video, and an album with Rhino Records, and are performing in LA music clubs such as Madame Wong's West and Club Lingerie.

As for Brian's tentative return to health, after the divorce he regressed again to the point where he weighed 311 pounds and had severe drug problems. "Carl came to me, and they asked my advice, and they all agreed that it was going to be either Brian was gonna be the next Elvis—gone—or get him back real strict and see if you could help him. So he's back on Dr. Landy's program." Marilyn sighs. Although her ex-husband is improving under Landy's program, she believes that he will never be the same. "Brian lost his innocence and spontaneity and his tenderness. Brian was a very, very, very tender person, but to him being tender was sissiness. Brian always felt that people would laugh at him 'cause he sang real high like a girl. That was just his voice naturally, and he loved singing like that. He always wanted a low voice and he had a hang-up about it. Now he's loud and boisterous. I don't particularly like that."

nita Pallenberg

BRIAN JONES;
KEITH RICHARDS

*"I always had my boyfriends on
the side. It was loneliness. I used
to introduce them to him."*

*A*lthough Anita Pallenberg has an impressive list of acting credits behind her—including roles in the films *Barbarella* and *Performance*—she is far better known for her real-life role as the woman who bewitched first Brian Jones, then Keith Richards of the Rolling Stones.

Anita's long and notorious association with the Stones began in 1965, when she managed to finagle her way backstage at one of their concerts in Munich. Right then and there, Brian Jones took a fancy to her, and soon they were rendezvousing for romantic weekends all over Europe. When, some months later, Brian, whose position within the group was crumbling, brought Anita to England to live with him, the arrival of this long-legged, multilingual Italian-born German beauty immediately elevated Brian's status with the others. In any case, Anita and Brian, with their identical bleached-blond Beatle-style bobs, were a mischievous pair: Anita persuaded Brian on one occasion to pose for the cover of a German magazine wearing a Nazi SS uniform while crushing a doll underfoot. But there was a dark side to Brian: He had a tendency to beat up his women. Eventually Anita grew tired of Brian's abusive ways and in 1967 fled into the sympathetic and willing arms of Keith Richards. That union—which lasted a dozen years or so—produced Marlon, now fifteen, and Dandelion Angela, twelve (a third child, Tara, died in 1976 at the age of two months).

At some point in their relationship, both Anita and Keith became heroin addicts, and it seemed like that whenever they got their names into the papers, it was because of one drug arrest or another. In 1977 Canadian customs officials found a heroin-encrusted spoon in Anita's luggage (and a package of Tic Tacs, which they confiscated for examination); this led to a raid on Keith's hotel room in Toronto, where police found an ounce of heroin. As a result, Keith kicked junk and managed to stay out of trouble. Anita was not so lucky. In 1979, a seventeen-year-old boy shot himself in her bed in the Westchester home that she shared with Keith. Disturbing as that incident was (Anita was eventually cleared of having any part in the boy's death), people seemed to be more shocked by the photographs of Anita taken as she was escorted from court: Vastly overweight and dull-eyed, Anita was virtually unrecognizable from her acting days.

Not long after that incident, Keith and Anita began to drift apart. From time to time, Keith was seen in the company of other women. Then he met freckle-faced American model Patti Hansen, and that was that. Keith and Patti married in December 1983.

Since there has been no news of Anita for some time, many people have assumed that she has become just another pathetic victim left behind by the Rolling Stones.

■ ■ ■

True or false: In 1985 Anita Pallenberg is:
(a) Fat
(b) A practicing black witch
(c) A hopeless junkie
(d) Happy, and in love with someone who is not even remotely connected with the Rolling Stones
   Answers:
(a) False. The Anita Pallenberg who arrives at the Plaza Hotel in New York for the interview is model-slim and looking quite glamorous in a full-length black-and-white fur coat. She has just been for a brisk walk in the cold December air around Central Park, and in fact, she looks downright healthy.

(b) False. Although Anita has always been interested in the occult ("I do believe in forces") and was, by her own admission, at one time "messed up about it," these days Anita is just sticking to reading about the stuff.

(c) False. Anita, it seems, has finally kicked the debilitating heroin habit she once shared with Keith. For a while, she even stopped drinking, and produces an Alcoholics Anonymous card from her wallet to prove it. "But I was too hyper, too active," she says. "I was annoying everybody. So I just have a drink once in a while."

(d) True. One of the first things to come out of Anita's mouth is that she is happy—"Which is something I didn't know, never." That's hard to believe: Anita can't seem to stop smiling, and her gaze is direct. And she is in love. "I met a guy who had nothing to do with the Rolling Stones or music," she says with a big smile on her face. "I have to have somebody to love. It keeps you going."

So much for the rumors. Now for the story:

Anita Pallenberg was a war baby. She was born in Rome in the middle of World War II at a time when Italy was being heavily attacked by the Nazis. Because of this, Anita says she remembers being in sort of a permanent state of shock all the time. "My dad had to go to Germany and my mom took us up in the mountains, up close to Austria. We drove through all the burning cities. My mom must have been mad, but she was just trying to get us away from the Nazis. So this is how I learned to walk and talk. I don't think I even spoke Italian or German—I talked in some terrible language."

So by the time Anita was eight and back living in Rome after the war, she felt much older than her years. "When I was eight, I felt like an eighty-year-old person. I felt wise, I felt the pain of everything weighing on me." And to add

to her troubles, Anita's older sister was a bully. "I was at
her mercy for many years." Anita points to the joints of
her fingers and says, rather dramatically, "She cut my fingers when I was about two months old so I couldn't suck
them anymore. She broke my arm. She sent me down a
hill on a sled. And I was tiny, rickety, a very bony little
girl. She just wanted to get rid of me." But one night Anita decided to take action against her sister. "I used to have
insomnia at night and used to share a bedroom, so I played
the flute under the covers. She was complaining, obviously, so I banged her on the head, and she passed out."
Anita smiles like a mischievous little girl. "So I finally found
out that she was vulnerable. And from then on I grew up
really wild. I skipped school very early on. I used to say
good-bye and then not go, so eventually they put me in a
live-in school in Germany."

At first, Anita liked it there. "My performance was really
good. I read Kafka at an early age and all the classics and
I wanted to study medicine." At some point, though, Anita lost interest in school. "I was precocious and I wasn't
happy, either. I just liked to go sailing and out into the
woods. They found me hitchhiking and taking bicycles out
into the wild. Skipping school, they kind of threw me out
of that school as well"—only half a year before she was set
to take her university entrance examinations. "I really
thought it was terribly unfair," says Anita, suddenly becoming indignant. Then after a pause, she seems to change
her mind. "Well, I must have deserved it somehow," she
says with a little shrug of her shoulders. Since university
was out of the question, Anita decided to go to art school
in Munich. "A real fun town. There I had my first sexual
encounter. I'm a late bloomer, I guess." As Anita tells it,
it was not a pleasant introduction to sex. What happened
was, one day Anita went to get some art books from a
friend. The friend, however, had mistakenly handed over
her books to a strange man. "I said, 'Well, I'll go pick them

up.' He tried to rape me. That was a big shock for me."
After that, Anita didn't go near men for quite some time.
"I went totally antimen," she says. "I found them very ob-
noxious, so I just ignored them." Which is not to say that
Anita led a chaste existence. "I went with women," says
Anita, with that impish smile of hers. "In Italy it's like a
pastime. It's in the summer when the sun shines out.
Everybody does it!"

By the time Anita was nineteen, she was, as she says
modestly, "quite attractive." Attractive enough, certainly,
to arouse the interests of film directors in Rome, who began to offer her parts in their movies. "I thought, 'Well, in
the summertime, when I'm not studying, I might get some
little role and not tell my parents.' And then my dad found
out and he said, 'You're just a slut.' So I left home, because I really didn't want to give in to what he was saying." By this time, Anita must have gotten over her fear
of men, because she had hooked up with an Italian artist
by the name of Mario Schifano (who, coincidentally, would
some years later have a fling with Marianne Faithfull, Mick
Jagger's girlfriend). "We were good pals and everything and
we decided to go to America and see Rauschenberg and all
the pop artists."

They arrived in New York in 1963, right about the time
of John F. Kennedy's assassination. Anita remembers how
somber the mood of the city was at that time, but she also
recalls how, in spite of that, she managed to have a good
time at jazz clubs and hanging out with artists like Jasper
Johns and Andy Warhol. Things with Schifano, however,
didn't work out, so Anita eventually went to work for an
Italian photographer who worked for *Vogue* and *Harper's
Bazaar*. Sometimes she would stand in for models who were
late or ill. Apparently, someone in a high place must have
liked Anita's look, because before she knew it, she was a
full-time model. Anita says she was never that thrilled with
being a model, though. "I've got straight hair, and in those

days you had to have curlers and false eyelashes, and I refused all that. And I never had a good relationship with photographers, I must say. I thought they were slightly male chauvinist. So I'd just walk out. My reputation was a bit odd, but I still used to make tons of money. The first money I made I went out to Paris to buy myself a snakeskin jacket." (Which she would later lose on the road with the Stones— "With my life-style, I lost everything, especially the things I liked," she says.)

In 1965 Anita went back to Europe and modeled all over the continent. She was in Munich on a fashion job when she read that the Stones were going to do a concert there. A photographer smuggled her backstage, where she met Brian Jones, the sensitive and musically gifted Stone who, by the age of twenty-three, had fathered three illegitimate children. And that was the beginning of Anita Pallenberg's long association with the Rolling Stones. For the next few months, Brian and Anita rendezvoused all over Europe. "When I think about it, in the early days it was kind of fun," says Anita. " 'I will meet you in that town,' and then I would fly by myself and I would see them in the other town. But then when things started to get bigger, I didn't enjoy the life-style at all. I didn't like the whole scene. Honestly, I can say now if I knew they'd become that famous, I'd have moved out and disappeared long before."

Within a short time, however, Anita was installed in Brian's house in London. The domestic situation there would not prove to be exactly harmonious. "I think Brian was a terrible person really," she says. "And I put up with a lot. I was really fascinated with his talent. Why I stuck first to Brian and then to Keith was because of the music. But all the side effects . . . he was a tortured personality, insecure as hell. He was ill very early on from when I met him. He was totally paranoiac." They argued, especially over things like Anita's career. "He didn't like the fact that I was working. So when I came home with this big fat script, he tore it in half. Jealousy. English people are odd in the head, you know? Eccentric. But I went on." Anita landed a role in German director Volker Schlöndorff's first fiction movie, *A Degree of Murder* (he went on to direct *The Tin Drum*) and talked Brian into doing the music for the movie. "That movie had success," says Anita. "It went on to Cannes Film Festival."

In spite of their collaboration, things between them were rapidly falling apart. Brian was drinking heavily and, as the story goes, could be terribly abusive. Finally, when Anita couldn't take his behavior anymore, she left him for Keith. "I found there was an enormous talent in Keith, and Keith was really a shy little guy in those days, couldn't come out of himself. And I had all this kind of Italian energy and outgoing personality, so it was really easy for me. And somehow it finally came out. Then he started to write songs and he started to sing them himself. I thought it was wonderful."

Would Anita say that she was the inspiration for some

of Keith's songs? "I couldn't say that," she answers. "I was writing songs with them. We wrote together 'Honky-Tonk Women' and 'You Can't Always Get What You Want.' " Anita also played critic: If she did not like their music, she was not afraid to say so to the Stones. "I'd always tell them, and to my amazement they would listen. Nobody else would. They were all yes-men. I call them 'shampoo people'—guys with three-piece suits and curlies." In general, she thinks that most of the Stones' hangers-on were afraid of her—"I've always done what I wanted, and that scared them. And I do have my temper."

Compared with Brian, Keith was a far easier person to live with, but still "Keith had the same problem as Brian with doing the movies," says Anita. "I got to do *Candy* in Rome, so I got to meet Marlon Brando. So Keith heard that Marlon Brando and I had a scene, so he took the first plane and he was out there. It was the same story, so eventually I tried to time it out to work where Keith was working. But he'd always stand me up. So eventually I gave up and I didn't show up on a couple of sets. And then I had kids, so I slowly moved out."

Anita's increasing dependence on drugs didn't exactly help her career, either. "We started to take acid and all that. That took about ten years out of my life—all that police stuff. Wherever I was, I was getting busted. For nothing! I got busted for Tic Tacs. Ridiculous. Very embarrassing, really," she says.

What got Anita into drugs in the first place was, she says, a combination of "loneliness and boredom." But she says it was her sense of discipline that kept her from self-destructing entirely. "I'm really amazingly German in that way," she says. "I think I had a notion of what excess is, so I never really took blindly. It's not like Marilyn Monroe, who forgets how many barbs she's taken. I couldn't do anything like that. *I* remember. But," she adds, her green eyes twinkling, "I think I know the art of falling over. And everybody seems to love it. Marianne [Faithfull] knows it some more. She knows it to perfection. I always was jealous how she used to get carried around. So why didn't they carry me around?"

Anita maintains that, throughout the roller-coaster years with the Stones, she and Keith were "always basically down-to-earth, keeping things very simple. All the other people can say what they want," she says, a little huffily. "The example I can say is my son [fifteen-year-old Marlon, who lives with her on Long Island]. He could be a snotty little kid and he's really down to earth. We lived together because Keith was always on the road, so we've been stuck together for years, and to see how he comes out, it's great. He's got no airs. He wants to be an archaeologist. For me, children are the best thing I ever had. Everybody was slashing me when I had Marlon, saying, 'You must be crazy to have children. How can you have a child on the road?' I thought it was better to be with the parents than by himself. Marlon learned to walk on stage, practically."

If Marlon thrived on the road, Keith and Anita's twelve-year-old daughter, Angela, did not. When the subject turns to her daughter, Anita sighs. "With her, I don't know. On the road, she used to go off by herself, pick up guys, bring them back—'Mommy, here.' Big guys. And I'd get really scared. And she'd go out of the hotel rooms, and I'd find her sitting on the lap of somebody. That's why I decided not to have her on the road anymore."

For now, Angela is being brought up by Keith's mom, Doris Richards, in England. Explains Anita, "I lost one child, right? So at the time when I lost him, I went through a heavy nervous breakdown. For about three months I was very upset. So Doris offered herself to look after her. Now the problem is she's keeping her in a shell. She seems to be more conscious of who she is, who Keith is. Like Marlon is Keith's mate, and they've always been mates, but it

seems to be more difficult with her. I meet Keith now and
talk about it and see what we can do. We're trying to re-
deem her."

Surprisingly, up until this point in the interview Anita
has not made a single reference to Mick Jagger, with whom
she reportedly had an affair on the set of *Performance*. When
this is brought to her attention, Anita smiles naughtily and
rubs her hands together, as if getting ready to tear him
apart. "From when I first met him, I saw Mick was in love
with Keith. It still is that way." In Anita's opinion, Mick
would like to *be* the way Keith is, "tough and macho." And
she says she helped him out with his acting when they
worked together on *Performance*. "He'd never done a movie
and he didn't know how to react to a camera at all. He had
a problem with it. I'd say, 'Relax!' " But she adds kindly,
"He's really quite sweet. He tries very hard. He's learned
a lot. He's become very cultured and very kind of gentle-
man-ish and well educated."

How did her lengthy relationship with Keith Richards
finally come to an end? Answers Anita, "The lawyers told
us we were no good for each other because of the drugs
and all that" (reportedly some people in the Stones' camp
blamed Anita for Keith's 1977 drug bust in Canada). "They
say we're a bad influence on each other." What Anita says
next is unexpected: "I always had my boyfriends on the
side! It was loneliness. I didn't think anything bad. I used
to introduce them to him. He met them all. But I think
the relationship was good, you know? It's not like Bianca
or Mick or Angie and David. It was nothing like that with
Keith. He's a very understanding, a very human person
and he appreciates home and he's really a rewarding person."

Anita took the breakup hard. "For a while it was a
nightmare," she says. "All my life was practically in the
same bag. So I couldn't really make out what was what. I
didn't know where my sanity was and where my identity

was at that point. I think it was the pain of love. That's what really hurts. Then I was still being harassed by the police and I really didn't find any reason. In London they tried to do that. I had to go to court again, and that really hurt me.

"I thought I could never have another love in my life," she continues. "I really thought, 'That's it.' I'm jaded. Where can you go after you've been in love with Keith Richards? What else is there? But it heals, it really does. You can actually get over a person. And then I met a guy who had nothing to do with the Rolling Stones or music," Anita purrs. "English people are wonderful. My cup of tea. It sounds like roses, doesn't it?"

It certainly does. And in other ways Anita's life has changed. For one thing, she is no longer a "preacher for the Rolling Stones sound and the Rolling Stones everything." (In fact, she thinks they should retire, "gracefully.") "Now I just started to discover other bands."

Lately she has been traveling all over the world because she feels that in spite of all her time on the road with the Stones, she never got to see it properly. "I went to all these airports and all these hotels, but I actually never really saw what I want to see. I tried to go myself, but I always got right in trouble because of security." And she wants to see the world soon "before it shuts down. You do understand that there's going to be a Third World War, don't you?"

Anita has no plans to return to acting, although she would like to try her hand at moviemaking again (she produced a movie in Italy in the sixties that starred Mick and Keith called *Human, Not Human* and won a couple of awards), this time a documentary on the life of Leni Riefenstahl, the official government photographer during the Third Reich.

Her relationship with Keith these days is quite amicable. "He doesn't ignore me. He doesn't put me through any bullshit [that is, alimony haggles] like Bianca. We already had so many legal hassles as it was. Who wants to go through more? He comes and visits and says, 'Hello,' brings goodies for Marlon, brings me tapes to play. He's mellowed out a lot. He's had lots of girlfriends from when we kind of split up, and I met them all. There was no way out of it. And I've been around him so long anyway. But Patti's [Hansen] the only one I think is okay. She takes care of him. I'm really happy, because you do feel you have to look after them. At least, that's the way I felt. I felt I had to protect him. He was flying so high in the music world. Anything material, anything that was going on, he couldn't recognize a face or anything."

That said, Anita begins to gather up her things, saying that her car is waiting out in front of the Plaza. Then, rummaging in her purse, she produces a package of Tic Tacs. "You see, I'm still on them," she jokes, and pops one into her mouth.

Gail Zappa

FRANK ZAPPA

> "*I remember Moon in the sixth grade coming home from school, and there was this girl who was really cute and popular who said, 'Why did your parents name you Moon?' and Moon said, 'Why did yours name you Debbie?'*"

*F*rank Zappa, composer/arranger/guitarist/bandleader and self-proclaimed genius, has been on the rock scene for almost two decades. His reputation varies widely from critic to critic: Sometimes he is praised for his fusion of classical and jazz music with rock and at other times criticized for writing childish and smutty songs with titles like "The Clap" and "Shove It Right In," as well as for his onstage capers like squirting his audiences with whipped cream from the stiff tail of a stuffed giraffe. Nevertheless, his place in the annals of rock and roll is assured.

Frank isn't the only Zappa to have made a name for himself in the entertainment world, however. In 1982, Frank's teenage daughter, Moon Unit, collaborated with her father on a record called "Valley Girl." Her rap on the record, which introduced such expressions as "Gag me with a spoon" and "Barf me out," made her a celebrity. And Frank's elder son, Dweezil, is embarking on a career in both rock music and in films. But there is at least one member of the Zappa household who has no intention of seeking the limelight: Gail Zappa, the wife of Frank since 1967 and the mother of his four children, has always stayed in the background and prefers to keep it that way, though she is certainly behind her children in whatever they want to do.

Gail and Frank met in Los Angeles in 1966, the year that Frank's first album, *Freak Out!* was released. He was flying into town after finishing his first promotional tour, and Gail had gone along with one of his friends to pick him up at the airport. At that time in her life, Gail was, by her own admission, an experienced groupie. Nevertheless, she was not prepared for the impact that Frank would have on her when he stepped off the plane. "I was just devastated," she says. "I didn't know what to do. It was like you were totally stripped of any preconceived notions about anything." For one thing, in person Frank was pretty imposing. "He probably scared the shit out of his mother too," laughs Gail.

But Frank couldn't have been *too* intimidating, because within a month Gail was living with him. The next year, she got pregnant by him. Two days before Moon Unit was born, they were married in a no-frills ceremony at City Hall in New York. (This was Frank's second marriage; his first had ended long before.) In lieu of a wedding ring, Frank bought Gail a little ballpoint pen from a machine for a dime that said "Congratulations from Mayor Lindsay" and pinned it to the front of her dress during the ceremony. (For the next few years, Frank would give Gail a pen or a pencil on their anniversary.) Today the Zappas and their children— Moon Unit, Dweezil, Ahmet Rodan, and Diva—live in movie-cowboy Tom Mix's Log Cabin Ranch in Los Angeles.

■ ■ ■

It is midday on a cool day in April. Beyond the green jailhouse gate that stands at the entrance to the Zappa property in the peaceful Hollywood Hills, there doesn't seem to be anyone at the Zappa household who isn't working diligently away at one task or another. Out in the flower garden, a young Englishman and Gail Zappa's mother are ripping out weeds. By the pool, someone who is introduced only as Stomach is laying down tiles. In the house the phones are constantly ringing, and a woman sorts through a huge pile of mail; one or two musicians are striding around with purposeful looks on their faces and guitar cases in hand. Frank Zappa, however, is nowhere in sight; one imagines him holed up in a room somewhere, frowning over music sheets. But as it turns out, he's still in bed. "He's on a biological clock," said Gail Zappa, smiling. She is sitting in what she calls the film room, a cool, dark room in the basement of the house that is packed with Frank's film-editing equipment and boxes of film marked with familiar Zappa titles like *200 Motels* and *Yellow Snow*.

In her black ruffled sundress, white ankle socks, sandals, and long, wispy blond hair, Gail looks a lot younger than what one would expect of someone who has been married eighteen years and raised four children. It seems other people think so, too. "All Moon's friends assure me that I don't look my age," says Gail. She goes on to admit that when she was Moon's age (sixteen), she was a very rebellious young woman when she was attending a "severely Catholic all-girls' school in London," where her father, a nuclear physicist, was working for the U.S. Navy. Daddy, it seems, had his heart set on his daughter going to college, but Gail had other plans. After graduation, she left home, moved into a flat with a girlfriend, and found a job as a secretary for the Office of Naval Research and Development. The year was 1962, and at that time in England a musical revolution was taking place. The Beatles had just had their first hit with "Love Me Do"/"P.S. I Love You," and groups like Gerry and the Pacemakers and the Searchers were beginning to get a lot of air play. After work Gail got pretty involved in the London music scene— "London had a lot of clubs and I was very social."

In 1965 Gail's father was transferred back to the States. That meant that Gail could no longer get a work visa, so she moved back with her family to New York. It was not long, though, before her former roommate in London, a girl by the name of Anya Butler (who would later marry Chris Hillman of the Byrds) came to Gail's rescue. Anya and Gail hitchhiked from New York to LA. And it was in LA that they "decided to be groupies for a while."

At that time in California, a lot of people who were Gail's

age were "freaks," who were indentifiable by their long hair and way-out clothes. "They were seen on the street together in groups for safety," Gail remembers. "Those were the days when if you drove down a street in a car, and another longhair was driving, you would wave. There were so few longhairs that were (a) making any money and (b) could afford to drive or (c) were showing themselves."

While Gail was not a full-fledged member of the freak scene ("but I was not straight"), she would participate in some freak activities, organized by "the acknowledged leader, Vito, and a guy named Carl Franzoni. We'd all get together and go to concerts and dance."

Another typical activity in that era was hitchhiking. "We went everywhere by hitchhiking!" says Gail, rolling her eyes. "What I did was very dangerous, but I think that that's what one does at that age." She also experimented with drugs. "And I would call it an experiment, because you wanna know what's going on and you're really dumb. Where are you going to get advice from? Every one of your peers is involved with drugs in some way, and it was all terribly cosmic, and you're in a time in your life when you're soul-searching and all that other corny crap."

As for attire, well, Gail remembers, "Anya and I didn't even bring a brassiere with us to California. I don't remember if we were the first, but I certainly remember bothering a lot of people." Though unlike many people at the time, Gail says she did not wear "a white John Lennon hat. And I never went near a go-go cage or burned a flag or helped anyone burn a draft card. I do remember people being arrested for wearing a flag, which most people can't even imagine."

But even almost-freaks have to eat, so the ever-resourceful Gail got a job working as a secretary for both the Whiskey A-Go-Go and the Trip, LA's most popular music clubs. There was a difference between the two, remembers Gail. "The Whiskey was a lot straighter and had

more of a drinking crowd. The Trip was famous because
it had all these outrageous acts. It was much more psychedelic."

When she is asked to list her credentials to groupiedom,
however, Gail laughs and suddenly becomes shy. "Well,"
she says, "we knew the Byrds and the Beach Boys—I'd say
Brian Wilson as a matter of fact. But," she continues, "I
think everyone who lived in Los Angeles and had anything to do with any groups in '65, '66, could be classified
as a groupie. I don't know if they knew what was moti-
vating them, but I think, how else do you get it off your
chest—this total fascination with the music business and
being part of it at the same time? It was almost religious
with the girls. They were the worshipers, and those guys
were like priests on the altar." This is not to say, however,
that there were not some sexual opportunists around at the
time. "There were a lot of girls who were in it for the castle in England. That was a prevailing dream: I must have
an English pop star and retire to one of those great houses
in England."

In those days, Gail didn't have any real career ambitions
for herself. "I played around with the idea of designing
clothes," she says. "I really felt like I was in a state of
waiting for whatever it was to present itself and just being
available for it when it came along."

That "it" turned out to be Frank. For Gail, meeting him
"was really a pretty shocking situation. He had every social disease I think that's possible. Well, no. This was before AIDS and herpes. Those were not the Top Forty
diseases to have at the time. Certainly the clap was and the
crabs. He was infested, and so was his hair. He hadn't taken
a bath for months. Or combed his hair. I think it was not
so much rock and roll and not so much the road as it is
that nobody was taking care of him. You can always spot
a bachelor!"

At the same time, Gail found Frank to be very "courteous. Most people come in and expect to find an ogre," she says, her voice suddenly becoming soft. "He's really kind to people. He has a very fierce personality. People ask me, 'How did you get to know Frank?' Well, I haven't. I think that's one of the things that is key to the relation-ship."

In her eighteen years of marriage, Gail says she's learned a thing or two about the occupational hazards of being with a rock star. "The biggest problems with rock-star mar-riages are drug abuse, insecurity, and confusion about what the fuck you're doing. I think that there are some women who should figure out right away, as soon as possible, that there are some things that you do not talk to your husband about—things that have to do with yourself and how you feel about the relationship that you're not sure about. It's not the job of your husband to answer your questions. He's not the authority. Marriage is a process of self-examina-tion."

Of course, throughout her marriage, Gail has had to live with the fact that groupies do not consider a rock star with a wedding ring off limits. ("I was a groupie. That's how I know.") And Frank has not exactly come out against grou-pies: In an article he wrote for *Life* magazine in 1968 he said, "Groupies . . . one of the most amazingly beautiful products of the sexual revolution." On the subject of grou-pies, Gail's voice rises a few decibels. "I hate it a lot. I've tried to sit there and 'Yes. I'm going to be calm, cool, and collected and not tear my hair out.' But the fact of the matter is I don't like it at all. I have psychic pictures of what hap-pens. There's no escaping it. I see it—I don't have to go there.

"There are a number of ways you can deal with it," she continues. "You can scream, which will get you nowhere. You can set up all kinds of barricades in your relationship, which doesn't help anything. What you ultimately have to face is being honest. I don't mean being honest with the

Gail Zappa with her daughter Diva.

person. I mean being honest with yourself to figure out what
your priorities are, and if you know what they are, you'll
be less likely to do anything to trip yourself up. You'll be
less hysterical if it's going to push somebody in the wrong
direction." Has anyone ever come out and said to Gail that
they've seen Frank with another woman? "Yeah, sure," she
answers. "All that stuff and anything else you can imagine
has happened. *I've* seen Frank with women." In those cases,
what does she do? Gail laughs. "You do what you do," she
says, with a little inscrutable smile, but does not elaborate.

Gail describes her brood—the children range in age from
four to sixteen—as a "pretty normal American family." That
may be, but one doesn't find names like Moon Unit or
Dweezil in your average American household. Not surprisingly, Gail says that the names of her children are largely
Frank's doing. "Frank gets to name them, I have them. I
had Moon when he was on tour in Europe, but as he was

going out the door, I said, 'Wait! What shall I name this baby?' Frank said, 'You can name her Moon or Motor- head." In the hospital after Gail had chosen the name Moon, a battery of nurses dropped by Gail's room to protest Gail's choice. "But my mother thought that Moon was a lovely old Chinese name," says Gail.

The second Zappa child (and first son) was given the same pet name that Frank had given to one of Gail's toes: Dwee- zil. The name of child number three, Ahmet, was a name for an imaginary person "we always had hanging around back when we had no one on our payroll. We'd snap our fingers and say, 'Ahmet? Dishes. Coffee, please.' He's also named after a Japanese monster, 'Rodan.' " Diva got the name she has because as a newborn baby, she screamed her head off. "And it turns out that Diva has this incredi- ble voice and she can knock you over from a distance of thirty feet."

So far, says Gail, all four children have wanted to change their names. "Moon wanted to change hers to Beauty Heart. And [horror creeps into Gail's voice] Ahmet wanted to change his to *Rick*. They've had their share of difficulties, but they've really handled it throughout their lives well. I remember Moon in the sixth grade coming home from school, and there was this girl who was really cute and popular and really shit who said, 'Why did your parents name you Moon?' and Moon said, 'Why did yours name you Debbie?'

"The best quote I've read about the names so far is in an interview that Frank did for a Columbus paper and it said something about how the kids didn't like their names and it was always a problem for them when they were growing up but they're going to find out if they haven't already that it's not the first part of the name that's going to give them trouble, it's the last."

After the success of the record "Valley Girl" in 1982, Moon (who emerges from her room briefly in T-shirt and

shorts and bare feet and turns out to be surprisingly shy),
Gail confides, found it very difficult to relate to her classmates and the activities at high school, so she quit to study
acting—a decision that does not appear to upset Gail. "Education in this country sucks," she says. "Moon earned the
right to make that decision for herself. She's very bright.
She really worked hard in high school, and she took the
high school equivalency exam.

"And she's a great actress," Gail says with motherly pride.
"Moon has a remarkable ability to express an overview and
to develop these characters, which she can project. She's
got a great sense of humor—it's really twisted."

Fourteen-year-old Dweezil plays the guitar and hopes to
follow his father in his choice of career. "He's working on
putting an album together. He's listening to all of Frank's
old records and a lot of classical music. He's tracing his-
torical roots and he's beginning to make musical connec-
tions." Dweezil already has one single behind him, entitled,
"My Mother Is a Space Cadet." Although Dweezil told his
mom that the title was meant to be general, Gail thinks
otherwise. "Certainly there were some things in there that
were inspired by my activities, like reading magazines and
being numb," she says. "When I get lost in print material—Frank says 'trapped by print material'—that's when
they'll go, 'Ah, she's reading a magazine. Let's go ask her
if we can go somewhere and she'll say yes because she's
not listening.' "

Gail calls herself a "professional mom," which is what
she had decided to be very early on in her marriage. "I
decided instinctually that we were going to have a lot of
problems in the future because when our kids are our age,
there's going to continue to be more of *us*. They're all going
out and taking a bunch of drugs anyway, and you know
you're living in a society that's creating a bunch of mu-
tants. I thought, 'Fuck this shit. The earth needs all the
help it can get.' "

Gail has no desire to go out and get a nine-to-five job. "Frank would have seriously questioned it. And I think there's a real problem today that women feel compelled to have jobs," she says. "I think if most women sat down and asked themselves why in hell they want to work—why do they want to wear that suit? Why do they want to carry that briefcase? What the fuck does it mean? I think it means that they're competing with their husbands; they have to have some status in their marriage. I don't know why they're not at home taking care of the kids where they should be."

Gail hastens to add that the above "is not a philosophy that Frank and I have discussed. Frank and I try to talk to each other as little as possible. We make an effort not to speak." Why? "Because there's really nothing to talk about unless something isn't okay. Because I do my job, and he does his, and my job is real different. I wouldn't want his job in a million years. It's just such hard work. He's so uncompromising. If it's impossible, he'll do it." A part of Gail's job, however, is making sure that everything runs smoothly for Frank, from day to day. "It's the boring stuff, like following up on the details, like set up an interview at a certain time or make their travel arrangements in a certain way. Mostly you just block for Frank so that all he has to do is do what he does with not too many distractions.

"It's a real job living with Frank, and I'm sure it's the same for him with me. Though I probably provide a certain amount of amusement," she says. "Sometimes he just rolls his eyes. Sometimes he laughs, but probably he's laughing more at me, whereas I'm laughing at something he's said. And I cook for him. He loves it when I cook. I've learned to cheat. I throw things together real quick and I pretend I was working for hours on this. Musicians are notorious. They can't wait. You have to feed them *now*."

As Gail talks, the bass player in Frank's band pokes his head into the film room. Gail asks him if he needs a ride to the airport, but he says no and disappears. Ask Gail her opinion of rock musicians today and she shrugs. "As a rule, musicians are not fun," she says. "The best of them are characters in their own right. They've developed a style and personality that it is possible for you to get off on. Most of them take themselves so seriously. In the sixties the thing that I thought was the downfall of most groups is that they thought they were really doing something [her voice gets cynical]—really making a statement. And they were out there night after night playing to audiences of thirteen- and fourteen-year-old girls. How can you get any satisfaction out of that if you are a mature, responsible male? You can't go on deluding yourself. Some people did by taking vast quantities of drugs. Then they go get these ladies to hang on their arm and they're selling another something to a bunch of thirteen-year-olds. This business is about image. The music business has nothing to do with music anymore."

Patricia Kennealy

JIM MORRISON

"I told him once that I thought he was the shiest person that I'd ever met and that he had to create a sensation as a sort of cover up. He thought that was just incredibly perceptive and very mean of me to say so."

*I*n 1969, Patricia Kennealy, a young rock journalist for a magazine called *Jazz & Pop*, was assigned to interview the Doors. Patricia had heard some outrageous stories about Jim Morrison, the lead singer for the group and former UCLA film school grad student who had become something of a cult hero with fans because of his provocative onstage posing (nearly always in leather pants!) and his offstage reputation as a heavy-drinking mad poet. But when Patricia found herself actually face to face with Morrison, she was impressed with his charming good manners and intelligence. After her interview with him and the other three members of the Doors came out in the magazine, Jim sent Patricia a letter saying how much he liked the article. A friendship was struck: From time to time Jim would call Patricia at the magazine or send letters, or they would get together for dinner when he came to New York.

Eventually, the friendship evolved into romance. Patricia was twenty-two; Jim, twenty-five. "We were just babies," Patricia says now. "And I was this total convent flower. It was all as inevitable as a fairy tale—like falling in love with King Arthur, or maybe it was more like falling in love with Darth Vader. He was a lover *and* an adversary."

But complications set in rather quickly. For one thing, Jim was still seeing his longtime girlfriend Pamela Courson, and his behavior was becoming increasingly self-destructive. The affair, which had started so promisingly, ended rather badly. Patricia sums up what went wrong in this way: "It was like starting to make a bridge from two different ends, and then when you got to the middle, they didn't meet."

Jim Morrison was found dead—of heart failure, as the story goes—in a bathtub in Paris in 1971. His girlfriend Pamela, who was with him when he died, would herself die of a heroin overdose three years later.

■ ■ ■

Patricia Kennealy is excited. Her first book, which she describes as "science fiction fantasy," is about to be published, and work on her second book is already well under way. Still, she is a little worried that in the interview she might come across as sounding like her life stopped after Jim Morrison. "The last thing I want is to come across like some sort of rock-era Miss Havisham, sitting in her cobwebbed room with her dusty memories and her old Fillmore programs," she says. Well, certainly judging from the decor of Patricia's East Village apartment—sort of medieval gothic—it does not appear that she has been doing much mooning. Granted, there are one or two Morrison posters, but for the most part the place is crammed with swords, chalices, crowns, masks, and even a highbacked carved bishop's chair. All this, coupled with Patricia's rather Old World looks—fair, fair skin and a mass of thick red hair, and a black cape—makes Patricia seem light-years away from being in any way remotely connected to the rock world, let alone Jim Morrison.

But the fact is back in 1967, as a writer/editor for *Jazz & Pop*, Patricia, at a very young age, was interviewing major groups like the Jefferson Airplane. *Jazz & Pop*, it seems, was a well-respected magazine run totally by women— "Rather unusual for that time," says Patricia. "Pauline Rivelli, who started it, was an extremely tough cookie. But it was really strange; the women writers a lot of times got tarred with the groupie brush when they would go and talk to people. The musicians were used to being pursued on the road, with groupies throwing themselves at them from

all directions. So they figured you were a total slut." Robert Plant, she remembers, was a prime example. "I was
backstage at the Fillmore, and, God, he was unbelievably
rude. I had a lace pantsuit on—perhaps"—Patricia says with
a smile—"he might have had a reason for thinking me a
person of easy virtue. He said, 'Hey, you in the lace nigh-
tie—come over here and sit on me lap!' We always got
propositioned. You had to have a hook of some kind to get
people to take you seriously." Indeed, Patricia was so incensed by musicians' treatment of women writers that she
spoke out against it in a column entitled "Rock Around the
Cock." She wrote, ". . . I tire even more of going out to
do an interview and being genteely condescended to as not
much more than a particularly well-connected groupie . . .
and then . . . having to watch the interviewee male drop
his drink at a perfectly ordinary remark as to, oh, the influence of eighteenth-century Irish-Scottish ballads on
his work . . ."

Needless to say, Patricia did not develop any great respect for musicians. "I just had incredible contempt for
them. They were idiots, they were morons. They are totally irresponsible. Musicians just seem to be flakier than
everybody else because they're always off somewhere." So
out of all the musicians she'd met through her work, there
was no one who sparked a personal interest in her. "There
just never seemed to be anybody who was bright and interesting enough."

Until she met Morrison. Patricia had been a fan of the
Doors ever since she had seen them at a performance in
Forest Hills in 1967. ("They were second on the bill to Si-
mon and Garfunkle.") But up until the time she was assigned to interview the Doors at the Plaza Hotel in 1969,
she'd never heard anything particularly good about Jim
Morrison as a person. "It was like Byron—he's mad, bad,
and dangerous to know." On the day of the interview, Patricia's expectations of Jim were reinforced, when, on her
way up to his suite, she overheard some groupies telling

stories "about how he would stick a needle in his eye—the point was that he was doing so much acid that his pupils were so dilated that it didn't hurt." So imagine, then, Patricia's surprise when she entered the suite and Jim rose to his feet. "He had such good manners," she remembers. "I was knocked out, 'cause you don't really meet good manners much among rock and roll people. And then, when we shook hands, there were just sparks! He loved it. It was just perfect."

Good manners were all well and good, but what really astonished Patricia was the fact that Jim took her very seriously as an interviewer. "He seemed to treat most people who came to talk to him like that. You didn't have to prove anything to him; he accepted you as you were." She also discovered during the course of the interview that Jim was highly intelligent (his reported IQ of 149 was "not as high as mine, but high enough," she says wryly). "He was extremely well read. We talked about music and about literature and writing."

After Patricia's interview came out in *Jazz & Pop*, Jim sent her a thank-you note, which Patricia produces from a box. It reads as follows:

Dear Pat
I want to thank you for the fine article which I consider the most brilliant witty and amusing. [sic] You should write fiction (I don't mean that as a slam) (Honest) Let me hear from you sometime. Please.

Yours truly
J. Morrison

After that, Patricia and Jim started writing back and forth. "It was all very innocent. His letters were just chatty letters about what they were doing, where they were going on tour, books that I might be interested in."

From time to time, Patricia would run into Jim at concerts. Then, some months later, Patricia was invited to dinner with Jim and his off-again, on-again girlfriend Pamela Courson. "I really did like her," says Patricia. "She was nice. She wasn't an incredibly towering intellect, but she seemed very sweet and very pretty, very California." In spite of Pamela's presence, however, there was something going on between Jim and Patricia. "The vibes at that table," she says, "were not to be believed. I just knew something was building up. I think we both knew from that dinner on, but I didn't know where it was going to get started."

The next time Patricia saw him was in May 1970, in Philadelphia. "That's when everything really started. They were playing there and we saw each other backstage." Patricia, it seems, had just written a not entirely flattering review of Jim's collection of notes and poems published under the name *The Lords and the New Creatures*. "Apparently it incensed him so that he sent me a telegram postmarked three o'clock in the morning from LA. A friend of ours from Elektra said that he couldn't get over the review, because it was the first review anybody'd really done of him as his work and not as him as a person. I think he was a little tweaked because it was a very accurate review."

But when they saw each other in Philly, all was forgiven, and two days later in New York the romance officially began. Asked to describe the setting, Patricia seems to have a hard time parting with the memories she seems to have stored away in a secret, special place. "We went to the Ginger Man on the West Side," she recalls almost nervously. "It was springtime and it was just so incredibly romantic. Nobody could eat because we were too excited." She was not, however, so totally swept off her feet that she couldn't bring up the subject of the status of Jim's relationship with Pamela. "He told me it was totally finished with her, which was the only way I would have started up with him, because I have scruples. He swore that they had broken up, that it was a poisoned relationship. He said it was half pity and half habit that had kept them together all this time. It was probably true when he said it, but he was just one of those people who changed his mind a lot," muses Patricia. "You never knew where you were. There was no consistency but inconsistency."

At any rate, after lunch the pair went for a walk in Central Park. They sat on the grass, Jim with his head in Patricia's lap. They ended up spending the whole day together. The next day, they went to a Jefferson Airplane concert ("He thought it was incredibly tedious and boring"), and afterward they went back to Patricia's apartment to listen to records. "He had his head in my lap and he said, 'Do you want me to stay the night and keep you company?' And I said, 'Well, if you understand it's not obligatory.' That surprised him. He said, 'No, it isn't.' " There is a long pause. "It was very nice," Patricia says shyly. "He was very sweet."

Jim, Patricia was soon to discover, was not as secure with her as one might think. "He could be extremely jealous. He would be full of questions about 'Who's my competition?' The first time he came to my house here, he was all over the house looking for men's clothing.

"Jim didn't believe that I really liked him," she continues. "He was always asking for reassurance: 'Why are you with me?' He didn't believe it after the first morning we woke up here after he spent the night here for the first time. I was just looking at him and smiling quietly to myself, and he woke up and we started to talk. During the course of the conversation I said something like, 'I really like you enormously.' And this incredible look of pleased surprise comes over his face. And he said, 'Well, no, I didn't know. I just figured if you didn't want me around, you'd let me know.' "

In the relationship, says Patricia, Jim gave "insofar as he was able to. He was very afraid to open himself up with people. He was real scared to do that, and I think that's why he had so many problems. A lot of the personality problem had to do with alcoholism, which prevented him from doing so. But he poured his guts out in his poetry and onstage. It's harder when your audience is just one person and your bodies are naked and your souls are naked and you have to perform in all senses."

What, then, did she get from being with Jim? Patricia thinks for a minute before answering. "That's a hard one. He just made me very happy in spite of all the bullshit. He could be the unadulterated creep, the pigman of LA. He could be incredibly cruel. I don't know how he made me happy." There is a pause. Then she says, "He was extremely affectionate—always holding hands in public—extremely romantic. He brought me peonies when he came over once. He gave me this gorgeous emerald ring, which I keep in the bank." She points to her aquamarine earrings. "He gave me these. He was very deep. He was always very interested in finding out what other people thought, how they thought, what they thought about, what they liked to read. I guess he got tired of always being the one doing all the talking. I think his curiosity would have been the one thing to save him. It just didn't happen enough."

As Patricia got to know Jim better, she also noticed this about him: "With people, he was whatever they expected him to be. Some people said he was almost kind of a mirror, just reflecting whatever you were. If you were expecting him to be the prince of darkness, he would oblige you." A lot of that, Patricia thinks, had to do with shyness. "I told him once that I thought he was the shiest person that I'd ever met and that he had to create a sensation as a sort of cover up. He thought that was just incredibly perceptive and very mean of me to say so."

In Patricia's eyes, the high point of her romance with Jim was when they were married in a Wiccan, or witch ceremony in her apartment on Midsummer's Night in 1979. Patricia, it seems, was involved with witchcraft. "It's not satanism," she is quick to say. "It's basically a mother religion, but there is also a god figure, a horned god of the hunt." Jim apparently was intrigued with all this, and it was he who suggested that they have the Wiccan wedding ceremony. So they were married by a high priest and priestess of the Celtic coven, who could have made the marriage legal, only Jim and Patricia didn't bother to get a license. "We just did the ceremony, which is binding a lot longer than till death do us part. It's a karmic sort of thing that links people through further reincarnations."

The ceremony itself involved "all kinds of rituals and candles and vows." Jim and Patricia, clad in black robes, stood inside a magical circle that had been cast with a sword. Four candles had been placed in four corners of the room.

Then, each of them made a slight cut on their wrists with the sacred ritual knife. "It was very dramatic," says Patricia. Then Jim gave Patricia a silver Irish *claddagh* wedding ring that has two hands holding a heart with a crown on top of it. Patricia doesn't know how seriously Jim took the ceremony ("probably not too seriously"), but to her, going through with the ceremony was "like being validated the way I wanted to be. It was a very private thing for me, a bond I wanted to make with this person."

Unfortunately, it was all downhill after that. First, Patricia discovered that she was pregnant. "It was an accident—the old diaphragm." And at this point, Jim was having his own troubles: He was in Miami facing charges for "exhibiting lewd and lascivious behavior by exposing his private parts and by simulating masturbation and oral copulation onstage." But they agreed that they had to talk, and Patricia flew down to Miami to meet with him. On her way there, Patricia's mind did flipflops. "I thought, 'Oh, my God, this kid is going to be a god. How could it not be? But then I thought, gods have to eat and go to school. You always have to be there, and I'm not very good with kids.' "

In Miami any hopes Patricia harbored of Jim wanting her child were dashed. "Jim was really cold," she says. "It was like he really didn't need this. He just didn't want to talk about it for the longest time. He just had all this other stuff. It took a couple of days before we started to talk about it." Then when they started to talk, Jim told Patricia that "if I had the kid, it would just ruin our relationship as far as he was concerned." "Maybe," muses Patricia, "it had something to do with the twenty paternity suits against him."

In the end, they decided that Patricia would have an abortion. Patricia flew back to New York, with Jim promising that he would be there to hold her hand throughout the operation.

As it turned out, he didn't show. He didn't even call, although Patricia learned later that he did call a couple of her friends to inquire after her welfare. "Jim could have handled it a lot better than he did," says Patricia, an understatement if there ever was one. Why didn't he come through for her? "I don't think he was good at adversity," she replies. "As soon as a relationship got trying, he would get crazy and run away from it. I used to think, when things got really hairy, 'Well, doesn't he want to keep me?' Apparently not, if it means work."

After Patricia got out of the hospital, she was, in her words, "a complete wreck." So she wrote a letter to Jim, which she decided to deliver in person in Los Angeles. "He was staying at the Chateau. I went there, left him a note, and nailed it to his desk with a little dagger with a little skull on top of it. I thought it would get his attention, and it certainly did. He called me that afternoon."

In California, Patricia stayed with Jim's former publicist, Diane Gardiner. In the apartment above lived Jim's Pamela. Naturally, in that setup, things were bound to get a little crazy. "I was at Diane's, and Jim had promised to come over. The phone rang at Diane's, and it was for Pamela 'cause she didn't have a phone. They asked me to go upstairs and get her. I was wondering when this was going to happen. So I went upstairs and got her. She opened the door and she was naked to the waist." And she was also, according to Patricia, "completely 'luded out on downers, just completely wasted. So I said, 'I'm going to tell you a few things' and then we started talking." Patricia proceeded to tell Pamela "everything." Why did she have the showdown? "I was mad," Patricia answers. "I also wanted some insight on why he was with her sometimes and with me other times. It was," she says, "a very nice little talk. It seemed so modern, so civilized. She said she thought it would have been a good idea if I'd had the baby. Then she said, 'Of course Jim wouldn't have given you any money or anything,' " which Patricia thought was a little mean.

In the midst of all this, Jim arrived. "He came in and said, 'Interesting stuff going on.' He thought it was just the most amusing thing. But he was unsure of himself and nervous, though."

Patricia immediately lit into him. "I was just so angry and upset from the abortion, and he said, 'Oh, I know, it was unforgivable. I'm a rotten person.' Of course I fell for it. We just sat there and talked. And then Pamela was there, and it was so strained. And then she just went upstairs in tears because he was staying with me, which I thought was very cruel of him. We ended up sleeping on the floor at Diane's place, and Pamela came in the next morning and found us there. He thought it was so funny. He said, 'I'm never going to hear the end of this.' I think he was losing all sense of judgment at this point. Our relationship had gotten so weird with all this other stuff."

This was not the first time Jim had played Patricia off another woman. "One time we were up at the hotel in New York, and there was this very strange woman who was following him around. She had just been released from a mental hospital, where he had corresponded with her. Her name was Joanna. She was hanging around the hotel, and it was the most bizarre thing because he had told *me* to meet him at the hotel. I went down to the lobby, and there was this person waiting for him. She said, 'He's not here.' He had sent her a telegram saying that he was going to be in New York. He said he felt sorry for her and knew she'd been in the hospital and that she was a big Doors fan. Finally he showed up and took one look at her and one look at me and said, 'I wouldn't have missed this for the world.' Then we all went to the movies. It was strange—he would totally ignore anything she said and would make an exaggerated effort to lean over and pay attention to me. It was cruel, and she was getting frantic." The next day, Jim and

Patricia discovered her outside his hotel room door, kicking and screaming that she wanted a divorce and that Mick Jagger was really the one. Eventually she got tired of kicking the door and left. Patricia thought Jim's behavior was cruel. "You don't send a telegram to someone and then do that. He liked to play people off one another and sit back and watch the fireworks."

In California, Patricia stayed around for a week. A couple of months later she was back. When she saw Jim this time, "He was completely falling apart." Joplin, Hendrix, and Brian Jones had all died their tragic deaths, and Patricia remembers Jim "running around telling everybody that he was going to be the next one." Patricia somehow knew he was right. "The atoms weren't going around the nucleus. It was like it wasn't him anymore. The dark side was taking over. There seemed to be less of a distinction between the public and the private. There was some very strange psychological stuff going on. And he was drinking extremely heavily."

As if that weren't enough, the friend with whom Patricia was staying in LA turned out to have a crush on Jim. In turn Jim's "roving eye had been caught, so I was very annoyed about that. And I ended up in a fistfight. It was unbelievable. The three of us were sitting on a couch, and she was unbuttoning his shirt. He was loving it. But I got mad at her. I'd been with him for a week, and he'd been so loving and attentive—it was more presents and 'I love you this and I love you that' and 'I'm going to go to Paris with Pamela but that's only to get rid of her.' He said, 'I'm going to be with you in New York in the fall, and we'll get a place.' I believed this! But I dragged that girl into the bathroom, beat the shit out of her, dragged her into the hall and then threw her down a flight of stairs. I can't believe I didn't kill her. I really did see red. It was horrible, but wonderful. I was mad at him and I couldn't beat him up, so I beat up her."

And what was Jim doing throughout the fracas? "He was asleep on the couch. Completely sodden. It was like he was dead already. He was just lying stretched out on the couch with his hands crossed, and the couch was a big high dark couch and it looked just like a coffin. And his face was all green, waxy. And I bent over to kiss him, and it was like bending over to kiss a corpse. That was the end of it for us. I knew I'd never see him again."

Soon after, Jim joined Pamela in Paris. Patricia was furious when she heard the news. "I take my sword out and slice up pillows when I'm mad, and there were quite a few pillows that were decapitated at that time."

Then she had a dream.

"Jim was standing at the foot of the bed. He didn't have a beard, which he had shaved off before he went to Paris, but I didn't know about it at the time. He just stood there and he was so real. I could almost smell him, his hair, the way his clothes smelled. He was just there and he bent down as if he were going to kiss me and he was just gone. Then when I woke up, my wedding ring was on my other finger. It was off my left hand and was on my right hand. I don't know how you can get a ring off your finger in the middle of the night. It's very hard to get off."

After the dream, Patricia told her friends that there was something very wrong with Jim in Paris. Ten days later Patricia learned that Jim had died. "A friend of mine called me about three o'clock in the morning with the news. Jim had been dead a week." Patricia got the first plane to Paris and went straight to his grave. "When I was there, it was lovely. There was a little ring of scallop shells around the grave and somebody had made a little wooden cross. It's disgusting his grave now—they have all that graffiti."

In the years since Jim's death, new generations of music fans keep discovering the Doors. For Patricia, the continuing popularity of the Doors has been a little hard on her. "It's very nice that he's remembered and thought of as a great artist but to have to walk down the street and see people with Doors T-shirts is very painful."

She, for one, doesn't agree with those today who call Jim Morrison "The Grandfather of Punk." "All that stuff is really garbage," she says. "I think Jim would hate punk. He was intelligent; he was literate; he was musical. Punk is none of those things. It's extremely nihilistic. He was not nihilistic. He was self-destructive, but he was not a nihilist."

If Jim were alive today, would Patricia put up with all the stuff that Jim used to pull on her? "Never in a million years!" she answers vehemently. "No way. This wasn't any kind of liberating relationship! He called all the shots. And the worst part of being with him was that I never knew whether I was going to see him again. I never asked him, 'When am I going to see you again?' I was afraid to hear what he might say.

"If he showed up at the door today, which I sometimes fantasize about, with all this nonsense about 'well, he isn't really dead,' the first thing I would do is flatten him, like that girl in *Indiana Jones*."

Monika Dannemann

JIMI HENDRIX

"I've never seen him taking anything of drugs, nothing whatsoever."

*I*t has been fifteen years since American black rock guitarist Jimi Hendrix, who once electrified audiences with his wild stage act and unconventional guitar sounds, died at the age of twenty-seven when he suffocated on his own vomit during a barbiturate overdose, but if anything, Hendrix is more popular today than when he was alive. Since his death in 1970, virtually every note that he recorded has been released on over one hundred albums, and in some cities in Europe, Jimi Hendrix Information Centers have been established.

Part of the myth that continues to surround Hendrix is his legendary appetite for drugs and women. Rumor has it that he fathered many illegitimate children and had groupies stashed away in nearly every major city in the United States and Europe. One of the most famous Hendrix groupies, known only as Devon, herself died of a drug overdose less than two years after his death.

Nevertheless, German artist Monika Dannemann is one person who refuses to believe all of those stories of Jimi's indulgences. Monika had met Jimi while he was on tour in Germany in 1969. They hit it off and kept up a correspondence when he returned to the United States. They got together again in England in September 1970, just a few days before Jimi's death. Indeed, Monika was there when he died.

In the times they were together, Monika, who now lives in a seaside town in England, claims that she never saw Jimi do any drugs and that they were talking seriously about marriage. Whether Jimi successfully hid his womanizing

ways and drug habit from Monika or whether she was aware
of his ways but prefers not to speak ill of the dead is un-
certain. Still, the side of Jimi that Monika talks about in
the interview that follows is not one that is often presented, and for that reason, her story is interesting.

■ ■ ■

From the moment you step inside the thatched-roof house
where Monika Dannemann lives, it's quite obvious that the
spirit of Jimi Hendrix is still very much alive within her
heart and mind. Photos of Jimi—including ones taken by
Monika on his last day alive—are displayed in prominent
places. There are also a number of portraits of Jimi, painted
by Monika. One of these, which hangs in Monika's living
room directly across from an enormous gold Buddha,
painted ten years after Jimi's death, is really quite eerie. In
it, Monika has painted herself kneeling by a calm, clear pond
bending over to look at her reflection in the water. But it's
not Monika's face who is reflected back to her—it's Jimi
Hendrix. Then, as Monika begins to talk, it becomes clear
that with this picture she meant to demonstrate just how
spiritually close she was with Jimi when he was alive. "What
I noticed with him and me was that he was telepathic,"
she says, looking like a sort of mystical Gypsy hippie, in
her black velvet jacket and bellbottom slacks, with a head-
band holding her long fair hair in place. The picture of Jimi
encased in a star-shaped pendant that she wears about her
neck adds to the mystique. "Jimi could read what I was
thinking. He could actually pick up on certain subjects that
I was thinking in my mind and say, 'What about this and
this?' It happened all the time."

For Monika, it's funny to look back and remember that
she wasn't even the slightest bit interested when some
friends of hers approached her and asked if she wanted to
meet Jimi Hendrix when he came to play in her hometown of Düsseldorf in January 1969. Monika had seen Jimi

in concert before and saw that Jimi "was beautiful in gui-
tar-playing and composing, but as a person I didn't know
anything, and what I read in the newspapers didn't tell me
anything very good. Going by this, he was a very primitive person. Nothing for me!" And anyway, what did
Monika know about rock and roll musicians? Most of her
life had been wrapped up in her ice-skating career—going
for gold medals, competing in international championships. In fact, had it not been for the injuries that Monika
had received from car and skating accidents, she would have
been in Geneva at her job teaching skating and not in Düsseldorf at all when Jimi came to town.

But Monika's friends, who owned a disco in town and
badly wanted to get a promotional picture of Jimi at their
place, wanted Monika to stop by because she was the one
who had the best camera. Also, she spoke English better
than anybody else around. "After a discussion for a half an
hour, I finally agreed, but I was not at all interested to meet
Jimi," she says. "So I went in, and we sat down at the bar,
and then Jimi came in. He just sits next to me," she says,
very, very softly. "He talked to me for two hours, and
through that I noticed that the picture I had of him was
completely wrong; he was really very kind, intelligent, and
he really fascinated me.

"He first asks everything about me," she continues, "and
in ten minutes he asked me if I had a boyfriend—which I
did not at that time. He didn't believe me. Anyway, within
half an hour, he asked me if I would become his girlfriend.
I thought he was joking. And if I would come to England
and live with him and everything. And he kept on saying
these things. He really tried to push me. I was trying every
way to get around and change the subject, because it was
too quick for me."

After about two hours of this back and forth, a roadie
came by to inform Jimi that it was time to leave for Cologne, where Jimi was scheduled to play that evening. "So

Jimi asks me to come with him. And I was very puzzled because of the things he said to me, and also I realized he was completely different and I was fascinated. He really took me. I'd never met anybody who was such a gentleman as him. He would always take your lighter and light your cigarettes, open the door."

Apparently, Jimi was so convincing that Monika agreed to follow him to Cologne in her own car. "Normally I wouldn't be around this person," she says. "Just because somebody is famous, it doesn't mean I think this person is great. But what completely took me and why I fell in love was because he was a genuine person, so gentle and so kind and so loving to everybody and really tried to help everybody. He never seemed to think about himself." As an example, Monika says that Jimi was very interested from the beginning in what she planned to do with her own life. "I was explaining to him that I did skating teaching and that I was also interested in painting. So he wanted to see and he saw my paintings—at that time I was thinking maybe to go back to skating, I wasn't sure—but he said to me no way I should do anything but painting. He believed completely in my paintings and he started to do plans about my paintings and he wanted me to do paintings for his covers. Then, further in the future, for each lyric he wrote, he wanted me to do a painting for each lyric. He wanted to do in New York an exhibition. He gave me courage with my painting and he said, 'Keep on,' and he really loved them."

Watching Jimi perform for the second time in Cologne "really touched something in myself," says Monika. "He was just standing, not moving. The way he played the guitar—I couldn't believe how quickly he moved his fingers. It was fantastic, the music that came out of the guitar. I felt that his music was spiritual. With his music he was moving from one dimension to another. For some people, it completely changed their lives, the way they were

**Monika Dannemann with one of her
portraits of Jimi Hendrix.**

thinking. It touched them so strongly that they didn't know
anymore what was what."

Jimi's music and personality had the same impact on
Monika. "Through his teaching I completely changed," she
says. "He was the one who started to teach me and make
me understand all these spiritual things he knew. I see things
in a completely different way than I used to. And I used
to see them in the light of how you really get educated by
your parents or whatever. But he really made me completely free in the way that whatever people tell me—it
doesn't matter whether it's the government or the sys-
tem—I do not believe what they say, but I completely start
to check if what they say is right and what is really
behind.

"Also," she continues, "I never used to believe in incar-
nations and in karma or destiny—all these things he made

me start to believe. The people I knew, they were not spiritual at all, but when he started to talk, not only about incarnation but also the auras around people, he could also see the auras of people and the colors and he knew which color meant what. Somehow, when he said these things, I didn't doubt them."

In all, Monika was with Jimi on the road for one and a half weeks. For her, the experience was "very strange," she says. "I never liked it, because you never have any private life. No matter where you go, if it's a restaurant, a café, even in the hall of a hotel you meet other people, and they want to go out or just to talk with you. I personally didn't like it because after a certain time I did realize that there was a lot of people just wanting to be near Jimi, not because of him but only because he was famous. And they took a lot of liberties. For example, when we were in a restaurant, they would just come and sit at the table without asking, but not only that, order drinks and food and never pay. I've seen that so many times, and Jimi, he was far too gentle and quiet, he didn't like it but he could not say anything against them. First I saw it and I thought I must be mistaken. Then I asked Jimi, 'Why are you paying? Do you know them?' That was in the very beginning when I didn't know who he knew, and he said, 'No, I just met them today.' He knew what kind of people they were and he just didn't want any trouble. I thought it was a cheek."

Monika said this sort of thing happened over and over again. "For another example, in New York, he went to the studio, riding in a taxi. The driver recognized Jimi, and he said, 'I'm a bass player. I would like to come to the studio and play a bit with you.' And Jimi said, 'Well, if you're good enough, you can do it.' So the taxi driver came, another time, another day, and I tell you, he played for twelve hours and he was no good whatsoever, so Jimi had to erase the whole tapes. But Jimi didn't tell him to leave. Jimi, when he was watching him, realized that this guy had so much

fun and was so happy to be able to play that Jimi couldn't
spoil it. This is the way he was with many, many people."

"Another thing about Jimi," she continues, "in private
life, he was so different from his wild stage act. He was
very, very shy. You would never see him freak around.
For example, when we went to a restaurant, he asked me
to pay the bill. He didn't dare to do it. Another example,
one time he went shopping and he was buying some trousers and he asks me if I think they look nice and I said,
'Try them on and see.' So he came out again, and they
were quite tight, so he said, 'No, they're too tight. I cannot wear them.' I said, 'What? Naturally you can wear
them. They're not too tight.' And he really felt quite
ashamed being in these tight trousers."

According to Monika, Jimi also refused to dance in public. "He was too shy there, that people would watch him
and look at him."

When it is pointed out that Jimi didn't sound very shy
when he met Monika, she says, "It's funny, I asked him
after, and he said he never had done that before and he
said just the moment he had put his eyes on me he fell in
love. He said normally he would never have dared to do
it, but he said he knew he had to do it at that time, at that
moment, because he knew he would never see me again."

According to Monika, Jimi talked of marriage very early
on in the relationship. "He caught me by surprise there.
That was in '69 in March. We were somewhere in London, and he went into a jewelry shop and he bought two
rings, snake rings they were. And in the evening we went—
at that time Jimi was jamming a lot, he loved jamming—
and we went to the Speakeasy, and there he declared to
everybody that we were engaged. And he went everywhere around with me, all over the place, showing everybody about the rings and that we were wearing the rings
and that we were engaged."

For her part, Monika claims to have been embarrassed

about Jimi's public display of their affection. "First of all, I didn't know most of the people there, but he was so proud and so happy. At this time I didn't even think about it, because we had just met one and a half months ago."

In May 1969 Jimi returned to America. Monika had wanted to accompany him there, but, for two reasons, she says, he said no. "First, he said no because he wanted to break up with his management and he was a bit scared that maybe some people in the management would get very heavy with him and he was scared that they would do something to me. So he said he wanted to get this over with, and as soon as he got that together, he wanted me to come." That summer, Jimi told Monika on the phone that he had been kidnapped by two people, who held him in a warehouse. "He was really scared because he thought either they want to hurt him really badly or want to kill him. But after a certain time, he said, 'It's strange, they don't do anything to hurt me, they don't really say anything what they want.' What happened after a day or something, a couple of people from his management freed him. What Jimi told me was Mike Jeffrey, his manager, told him if they hadn't rescued him, he would be dead and he should be grateful, but Jimi started to think, and he thought the whole thing was strange how they just came in and freed him. He figured out that the whole thing was a setup by his management. So he was terrified that they might kidnap me because he knew that the moment they had me, he would have to do everything."

The other reason that Jimi didn't want Monika to come to America was because he was up against charges of heroin possession. In Monika's opinion, "That was another thing that was a setup—I heard it from a reporter that a girl at the airport [Toronto International, where customs officials found the drugs] gave it to Jimi as a present. Because he was late for the plane already, he just put it quick in, and they had to run to get a plane and there were drugs

there, and luckily because of her and she went and testi-
fied later in court, he got off."

To make up for the lengthy separation, Jimi called and
wrote Monika frequently. In his letters (in which he always addressed Monika as "Lotus," his pet name for her)
he told her of his struggle with his management over the
image he wanted to project. "He wanted to go more and
more spiritual with the music as well as with the lyrics and
he had a terrible fight with the management. In the beginning, he was playing very wild, 'Hey Joe,' 'Purple Haze,'
and in '68 he was trying not to play wild onstage anymore.
The reason he had done this, it was not his personality,
but he learned in America that people want not only to
hear something, they want to see something. The more
outrageous you are, the more they take notice, and the more
interest you get from these people. So that's why he started
this wild show, but he noticed in '68 that through this wild
show that he got a very bad image of being primitive. The
thing was with him, that the lyrics were very important.
He wanted to give certain messages to people through his
music, and these messages were spiritual. He realized that
people were misunderstanding all his lyrics because they
thought he was such a primitive person thinking only about
sex and drugs and whatever. For example, 'Purple Haze.'
Everybody right from the start claimed that Purple Haze
was purple heart—it was a drug. When he wrote that he
was not writing about purple heart, he was actually writing about an experience he had when he had an astral travel,
where there was this purple mist."

Given the fact that rumors of Jimi's escapades with
groupies were rampant when he was alive, was Monika at
all worried as to what he was up to when she wasn't around?
There is a long pause while Monika lights a cigarette. When
she begins to speak again, her words no longer come out
in a tumble, as they have been up until now. Very cau-
tiously and carefully she says, "Naturally there were a lot

of women around who were trying everything to get near to Jimi. I noticed this only after a certain time, because at the very beginning of the relationship he kept me completely away from everything, and through the whole time he tried to keep me away as much as possible from other people. *I* think for two reasons: First of all he wanted to be with me alone, because if we went outside, we didn't have any peace, but also he was very much a protective person.

"But we did go out, too, and I noticed that and I realized and I heard all the certain things—people saying this and this. Because they were trying to tell me certain gossip, so I started to question Jimi, but then he explained who was who and what was what. . . . Jimi showed me so much love that I was never worried." Monika pauses for quite a while before resuming speaking. "For him, the way he said it, I was everything to him, I never was scared in any way. He had so much people lying, and he did not lie. I never caught him lying in any way and I had complete trust in him. And the way he behaved when I was with him, there seemed to be nothing more important than me. It didn't matter on what was around him, he just concentrated on me. You only find that once. It is a dream. That's why I was never scared, because even when we didn't see each other, we were completely all the time in contact."

Monika and Jimi were at long last reunited in England in the summer of 1970. "It was far too long we were apart, and he immediately started to make arrangements and plans that we were getting married in October. He had already told his father in Seattle when he went to do a concert there in the summer that we were getting married. And he asked me to get a house in England in the country because he wanted to come and live in England. I did not finally get a house in the country, because he wanted it for our main home, and I wanted to choose it with him together. So I

Monika Dannemann in front of her thatched-roof house.

got a very beautiful flat in London for us, where we stayed
there, but because things were still going so heavy in
America, he checked in a hotel. But secretly we stayed in
our flat so that nobody knew where he was actually staying and that everybody would approach him from the hotel, which they did, and only in the last week did people
somehow find out where we were, because word always
seems to get around."

When Jimi died suddenly in Monika's flat on September
18, 1970, the coroner's report concluded that he had died
as the result of a drug overdose. Many were not surprised,
as it was largely assumed that Jimi was a habitual and heavy
user of drugs of all kinds—something that Monika hotly
denies and even goes so far as to say, "I've never seen him
taking anything of drugs, nothing whatsoever. As a person
Jimi was very much against drugs. Continuously I saw
people offering Jimi drugs and to all the musicians. It was

always very strange the way people reacted when he said
no. They could not understand it. Even after Jimi's death,
wherever I went, people were offering me drugs. I never
touched drugs. They did not believe me that I wouldn't
take them. They were so sure because I was with Jimi, and
Jimi they were so sure took drugs, that I had to take drugs
too." Monika lights another cigarette and continues.

"What Jimi did in 1967, he did take a few drugs—he had
taken LSD and he also was smoking hashish, but at the
end of '68 he completely stopped taking any LSD. He noticed that it was always very nice if you had a nice trip but
actually at the end of the day he didn't gain anything. It
was an interesting experience, but he would only go to a
certain point with these trips and that would be it. Spiritually he noticed that it was very bad. When he was naturally high without any drugs, he noticed that he could go
much further than with any trips. He only took it at the
beginning because it was so much in fashion, because every
musician was taking it and everybody was making jokes
about him not taking it, so he also started taking a few.
But he noticed that it was damaging in the way of the spiritual part. So he stopped it and was very much against it."

Monika thinks it was his management that was responsible for promoting Jimi's reputation as a big drug user.
"The management wanted very strongly for Jimi to have
the image of being a drug addict. They wanted all the time
that people would say he was drugged, drugged, drugged.
Another thing, Jimi, with the certain enemies he made,
because he was so spiritual, there were certain people who
did not want him to give this message, and certain people
thought it was dangerous in regard to the young people
to pick up on the spiritual message, because this message
that Jimi gave was very much against the establishment,
and it was first of all to recognize who you are and to do
the things you know are right, not what other people tell
you is right or wrong. And be completely free and be

very individual and not sheep of all the masses like most people are."

Coming as it did, Jimi's death was a complete shock for Monika. "I was prepared in no way, because I never thought about death in any way. We were looking for a house in the country near London, and at the same time he was talking about the baby we were going to have, the name and everything. When it happened, it just hit me, and I didn't know what was hitting me. It [her life] stopped for me for a few years—completely. Well, I never got over it, but just to be able to think straight, which made it worse, not just his death but what people wrote about him. This way they took advantage of his death, not having one bit of feeling for him.

"After Jimi's death I was not allowed to speak to nobody of the press for one and a half weeks because of the inquest. When I was able to speak, all over the papers, all over the world, was that Jimi died of drugs. Me not seeing any newspapers with all these stories of Jimi dying out of drugs and being in wild parties, which was ridiculous because we were only in our flat, and nobody was even coming into our flat. But by the time I wanted to say what really happened, how he really died, I went to newspapers and they said, 'We are sorry but we just printed this and we cannot just print now the opposite, but if you come back in a few months we will print it.' "

So Monika set out to write a book to set both the record straight on the circumstances surrounding Jimi's death and how he was trying to convey a spiritual message to the people. "That's when I got the telephone calls from Mike Jeffrey where he said if I would say one word of what I knew, I would not live much longer. There's something else—three times my flat in London, which was Jimi's and my flat, got broken in, and only papers were stolen. At that time I had a lot of jewelry and money, but nothing was taken except for my papers." Word of Jeffrey's reported harassment of Monika traveled through the music grapevine, she says. "One time I was in Düsseldorf, and I was with my brother in a discotheque, and there was Black Sabbath. They had a concert and they came in this disco with their manager, and the manager approached me and said, 'You know what's going on?' And I said, 'What do you mean?' He said, 'You know you have to be very careful. You should get some bodyguards.' I said, 'How do you know?' He said, 'Everybody knows.' He kept on calling me and saying you must get a bodyguard. He actually gave me the number of two guys, very heavy guys there were supposed to be. I never called them."

As it turned out, it wasn't necessary: The following year Mike Jeffrey died in a plane crash on his way to attend a court case involving Jimi. (Monika's book, incidentally, was never published.)

After Jimi's death, Monika flew out to Seattle to meet Jimi's family for the first time. "Through Jimi they did know everything about me and they were really beautiful, and now every year I go to America. Jimi's father is now married to a Japanese, and she has got children which are Japanese, mixed white, mixed black. Mr. Hendrix looks completely black, and his brother looks like a red Indian. If you're around them, there's no race anymore."

For some time after Jimi's death, Monika found it very difficult to listen to his music. "Tears were running down, especially because certain songs had a personal meaning with Jimi and me. Even now if I watch him in videos, I have to be in a very happy mood to be able to do it, because it really makes me unhappy. You see every little smile, every movement in the face, and you know exactly what it means." It took some years, but Monika says she has finally accepted that Jimi is really dead. "And I do believe that for Jimi he's very happy where he is. Nobody can hurt him anymore."

ngie Bowie

DAVID BOWIE

*"Zowie's got David's build
exactly, David's teeth, my jaw, my
eyes. I bet they burn into poor
David's face every time he looks
at him. My revenge is always
very sweet."*

*W*atching the impeccably tailored, clean-cut David Bowie in action today, it is hard to imagine that a little more than ten years ago he was the "Glitter King," prancing about onstage in dresses, plastic clogs, bizarre makeup, and flaming orange-dyed hair. In those days, it was not only onstage where Bowie was daring: In 1972, he openly admitted to a *Melody Maker* reporter that he was bisexual—and so was his wife, Angie. As a matter of fact, when he and his wife met, he recalled, "We were both laying the same bloke."

In contrast to David's somewhat jaded tone, Angie, while admitting the facts, is far more romantic in her description of their meeting. As Angie tells it in her autobiography, *Free Spirit*, in 1969 she was an aspiring American actress named Mary-Angela Barnet living in London and making ends meet by working as a travel agent in a tourist nightclub. One evening, her friend and occasional lover, Calvin Mark Lee, who headed the European offices of Mercury Records, took Angie to see *his* friend and occasional lover, a relatively unknown twenty-two-year-old singer named David Bowie, perform at the Roundhouse with his group, Feathers. Angie was captivated with Bowie. A few days later Calvin arranged for all three of them to meet at a Chinese restaurant. Afterward they went on to a club called the Speakeasy, where Angie and David danced the jive. Angie recalls, "After the Speakeasy, I felt totally different. I just knew David would figure importantly and irretrievably in my life: His whole nature and being was gentle and sensitive, but in his beautifully structured face I detected so much depth and definition to his character that it cried out to be explored." By the next night they were lovers.

Angie and David soon discovered that they had a lot in common. When Angie confessed to David that she had been expelled from Connecticut College for Women for having a lesbian affair, David was totally understanding. Angie recalls in her memoirs, "From his sympathetic attitude, I sensed that he must have had similar experiences, but I didn't press him to tell me."

Some months later David asked Angie to marry him, though he warned her not to expect anything conventional. His prediction was true enough: On the eve of their wedding, they spent the night with a mutual friend named Clare. "I had never been to bed with a man and a woman before," recalls Angie. "It promised to be something special. And it was." The next day—March 20, 1970—the accommodating Clare was a witness at Angie and David's wedding.

During their marriage, both David and Angie openly had extramarital affairs while at the same time pledging their undying love for each other. "We were not reluctant to share with others who came into our lives the love that David and I expressed for each other," wrote Angie. "We formed liaisons with those we worked with: singers, musicians, and artists from the footlights of the entertainment profession. . . . When David found a new friend, I rejoiced in his happiness, and likewise he in mine." The couple gave interviews to papers and went on talk shows to boast about their unconventional marriage, the purpose being, says Angie, "to show that a New Age of Enlightenment had dawned. An age in which bisexuals and homosexuals could find acceptance instead of living their lives in fear of ridicule and intimidation."

With the release of *Ziggy Stardust*, *Young Americans*, and *Heroes* in the seventies, David Bowie became a huge star with all the accoutrements—limos, champagne, and jet-set friends. Angie attended his sell-out performances in glittering gowns and furs. When David began to be seen on the arms of glamorous women like Bianca Jagger and Sabrina Guinness, Angie didn't protest. After all, she says, "How could I suddenly become an impassioned wife screaming abuse about infidelity when I myself had not practiced the marriage vows?" But somewhere along the line, their arrangement backfired: As David began to be more and more absent from home and for longer periods of time, Angie let suspicion and loneliness get the better of her. She resented the way gossip columnists would call her up and ask for a comment on David's latest girlfriend. Even more disturbing to Angie was her discovery that "David was sleeping with somebody that we had once made love with together." As a result, Angie became a drug addict and twice tried to kill herself with an overdose of sleeping pills. By the late seventies, the marriage was over, though divorce negotiations dragged on for two years. In the end, David was awarded custody of their son, Zowie (born in 1971), and Angie received a settlement of $50,000. Neither David nor Angie has remarried.

■ ■ ■

When Angie Bowie strides into the sleek and woody 103 Restaurant in New York's East Village one morning in May, everybody in the place stares. You can't really blame them: With her very short, ragged platinum-blond hair and a straight up-and-down boney figure, Angie Bowie's appearance is, like her ex-husband's, slightly androgynous. Maybe, like one of the waitresses there, the customers were just trying to figure out whether Angie was male or female.

At any rate, Angie herself pretends not to notice that all eyes are on her, though every word, every gesture of hers seems to be geared toward an audience. "Hello dah-ling!" she says, in a very pronounced Anglo-American accent as she plops herself down at one of the long wooden tables.

She hoists her foot up onto the table, hitches up the cuff of her black jean and yanks off a rather menacing-looking studded ankle collar. "God," she exclaims loudly, "I wore this bloody thing to bed last night!" By this time, the people at the next table have given up all pretext of reading their morning papers and are just out-and-out-gaping. Angie then proceeds to tell a long and involved story, accompanied by a lot of theatrical hand-waving, that has something to do with staying out late dancing at Heartbreak the night before and having too many whiskey sours and then not being able to find her way home in a cab.

In any case, in spite of the whiskey sours, Angie orders and devours a full breakfast. Between bites of scrambled egg, she explains that for the last six months she has been doing her own "national" poetry performance tour, appearing in small clubs and reciting her poetry to the backing of guest musicians. So far, says Angie, the critics' reception to her performances have been favorable. "I've been very lucky," she says, twirling the ankle collar in her fingers. "Fortunately, I command enough press attention that I do get reviewed, and fortunately, I'm good enough so that the reviews are great." Apparently, Angie is not chasing after fame—after all, she says, "I'm already real famous. I just intend to be very successful, a very good entertainer, very good at what I do. I'm also a video artist, and until I get to Germany and Japan where I'm doing some videos in conjunction with some really amazing young bands, this is just a scratching of the surface of what I had in mind."

Angie's dream has always been to make it on her own in the entertainment world—although back when she was married to David, she was shooting for a career in acting. But even with all the right contacts—she once met with Warren Beatty to discuss a supporting role in *Shampoo* (but her outfit, "tight pink pedal pushers, high stiletto heels, and a pale-green see-through bomber jacket" scared him off, she

Angie Bowie with two of her band members.

thinks) and got to test for the lead in the *Wonder Woman* television series—nothing much materialized in the way of offers. So Angie spent much of her ten year marriage acting as David's unofficial road manager. "Unfortunately, I lost my job when I got divorced," she says. "It was bloody inconvenient, too."

Without a husband to rely on financially and otherwise, Angie, who says she's been a dependent person all her life, was really lost. "I never worked in my life," she says. "My father took care of me, and when my father finished taking care of me, David took care of me. And then David stopped taking care of me, and then you think, 'Ay-hey. What do you do now? I have to do something here.' And I'm very spoiled and I'm used to going through enormous quantities of money, and where is that money going to come from? It's all economics and it's also real down-to-earth stuff. That's where the problem is. People don't make these provisions. I didn't do that. That's just the stupidity and the folly of marrying someone and in a naive, childlike way," she says, suddenly bitter, "really thinking it was going to be forever, instead of knowing that I should have already been planning, making provisions for what I was going to do. And I didn't do that. One minute I was sitting in a boat going down a river, and the next minute the boat was turned over and I was swimming for a bank. And then I thought, 'Wait a minute. The bank's too far away. Maybe I'll swim for the boat. No, I think I'm not going to make the boat. How about that rock over there?'

"You just don't know what you should head out for," she continues. "That's the only time that a situation was so difficult and noxious to me that I couldn't make the decisions fast enough. I knew I had to leave David, and it was really distasteful."

Somehow, Angie's survived the divorce. She credits a number of female friends with helping her pull through: "Women friends are really the strength and backbone, because I think they understand you so much better than someone who is of the male species. It's incredible to believe that genitalia can cause so much brainrot."

Which is not to say that Angie didn't have her men friends, too. After David, Angie took up with a certain Drew Blood (whose real name is Andrew Lipka), an Englishman of Polish descent by whom Angie has a three-and-a-half-year-old daughter, Stasha. Both her daughter and son, Zowie, says Angie, are very bright: "I breed champions, not slaves." Angie comes by her equestrian talk honestly: She and Drew have been partners in a horse-breeding ranch in Scottsdale, Arizona, for some years. (Though she and Drew, one gathers from Angie's veiled references, are no longer involved romantically.)

After Angie's mother died in late 1983, Angie decided to try her hand again in the entertainment world. "When your mother dies, you become very focused," she says. "She said, 'Look, I'm dying. Now you have to stop doing everything for other people and do what you want to do for yourself. Otherwise it's gonna be too late.' I'm just glad my mother said that because I'm *happy* now. I feel very stupid that I didn't do it earlier."

So Angie went to LA to become celebrity editor of a Larry Flynt–owned magazine called *The Rage: Rock and Roll Fashion with a Vengeance*. She was there three months. "I never had any problems or altercations with my boss, Althea Flynt, his wife, but I did have problems with the red tape, the sort of general hierarchy that ran it. So I'd resigned twice before, and the third time they accepted my resignation, and I thought, 'Right, that's good. It must be time to start the tour. Backing tracks are done. I'm off!' "

Marriage is not included in Angie's future plans. "Once was enough," she claims. "It suits you or it doesn't and it doesn't suit me. I'm very bad at conditioned reflexes. If anyone expects a reflex from me, I'll definitely do the opposite. And it's unfair for a person that's sort of fairly normal. The idea of signing a contract and then having to get out of it if something goes wrong I find just abhorrent. That's why I would never put myself in that situation again. You just decide that that type of pain is definitely not necessary and a bad one."

Angie doesn't quite take to the suggestion that rock and roll marriages tend to have more difficulties than others. "It depends. Like mining engineers' marriages [Angie's father was a mining engineer], they don't work either a lot of the time. But when you get outrageous dedication and martyrdom like my mother had, dedication to my father's career, then it works. It just depends on how many victims and martyrs you have married to the right people. I played martyr for a long time. I think it's something one tends to do when you don't want to deal with the reality of absence. I hated being away from my partner. I got so lonely. I really hated it."

Most of the time, though, Angie put up with David's long absences without a fuss, although occasionally she would resort to dramatic measures in the hopes of keeping David around. Like the time on their second night together, when David announced that he was going off to a rehearsal. Angie threw herself down a set of stairs in protest. Unfortunately for Angie that didn't stop David, who simply walked over her as she lay in a crumpled heap at the bottom of the stairs and went on his merry way.

In the years when they were married, Angie thinks that she was probably David's best critic as far as his music was concerned. "I'm extremely supportive and enthusiastic. I've never been a critic that would go, 'Oh, I don't like that.' I'm always like one of those wonderful teachers at school that goes, 'That's great, but did you think of . . . ?' And he knew that my ears listened with total love."

Angie hasn't seen David perform in "years," although from what she's heard of the new stuff, her opinion of it is that "the quality of the work of the songs isn't anywhere near as good as it used to be. I think there's something going on that's causing a computer malfunction in the creative process. He probably needs just a good new love affair or a kick up the behind. David's very creative. He hasn't lost anything. He's just being lazy. He has a great potential for true idleness. He can be truly idle, so he's probably just relaxing and taking a break. God knows he deserves the break, but when he writes when he's idle, I don't think it makes it. It still sells lots and lots and lots of millions and millions of tunes and records and radio play, so don't misunderstand me. It's just personally, I mean, 'Let's Dance.' Yeah, sure," Angie says, putting on a tired bored voice. "Okay. Let's dance. Dynamite tune," she says, her voice brimming with sarcasm. "Give me 'Width of a Circle' or 'Bewlay Brothers,' something I could really shake around in my teeth and really taste. I like something that moves me. The new stuff doesn't move me. It might move your feet onto the dance floor, but it definitely doesn't move my brain much except to think, 'Boy, are you ever bored.' "

Angie will concede, however, that her ex-husband is "a very astute businessman. You have to be that now, though I don't think he gets the pleasure out of entertaining as much as he used to because now it's an enormous business responsibility. You can't suddenly decide to go off and tour Germany because you fancy playing Heidelberg. The tax permutations of such an off-the-wall idea might be detrimental to your entire life. So you become much more a business institution, and you have so many people to consult and consider with every move you make."

Thirteen-year-old Zowie Bowie, David and Angie's only child, lives with his father in Switzerland but visits Angie during his school vacations. At the mention of her son (whose full name is Duncan Zowie Heywood Bowie) Angie's somewhat harsh and masculine voice suddenly turns soft and girlish and sweet. "I really adore him," she says. "It's a great thing when you finally see the maturity of everything that you wanted in a son and you suddenly realize that the need for husbands has disappeared forever. For a start, he's part of me, so I don't have to explain things to him. I think that's a thing women go through a lot with their husbands. They do understand that one should have a best friend and partner in a husband. That's sometimes very difficult when it's mixed with sexual connotations. 'Cause as soon as someone doesn't make you come or pisses you off in bed, you hold a grudge. That's a really nasty situation for a best friend. So with a son, because there's no sexual connotation, because he is a friend and part you and probably the better parts of the person that you originally married, it works perfectly. And there's no reason and no necessity to provide an excuse as to why they're so divine. It's your son, that's why."

Zowie, says Angie, resembles both of his parents. "He's got David's build exactly, David's teeth, my jaw, my eyes.

I bet they burn into David's face every time he looks at him." Angie narrows her ice-blue eyes and grins devilishly. "My revenge is always very sweet."

Angie will admit quite graciously, however, that Zowie has a wonderful father in David. "He's a great, great parent. He had a wonderful relationship with his own father— his father was public relations for Dr. Barnardo's Homes [for children] in England. As a teenager, David went and performed and did a lot of stuff with them. And he's a great mime and a great dancer, and so he's just wonderful for kids. He's so creative. He's like the Pied Piper, children just follow him. Probably the only fault that I could ever find with him is his schedule. I think Zowie wishes he had more time with him."

As the interview comes to an end, the talk turns to other people's music, and it seems an appropriate time to ask Angie if the Rolling Stones' song "Angie" is—as the rumor goes—about her. Angie looks down at her plate and smiles. "It's purported to be. There's a lot of songs written about me, and I don't know about it. It's not my place to know. It's . . . very flattering."

I *ngrid Croce*

JIM CROCE

*"I became less important as the
public became more important."*

*I*n 1973, Philadelphia-born folk-rock singer and song-writer Jim Croce was just beginning to get recognition for his music when he was killed in a plane crash in Natchi-toches, Louisiana. At the time of his death, he left behind a wife, Ingrid, and a two-year-old son, Adrian James (known as A.J.). In the months following his death, Ingrid saw three of Jim's albums go into the Top Twenty and several of his singles, such as "I Got a Name," go gold. She would not, however, see a penny of the royalties from the songs: They would all go to the record producers. As a result, Ingrid began a battle for the royalties soon after Jim's death, and at the time of the interview, she was still fighting for them.

The wear and tear of the legal battle hasn't wiped out Ingrid's good memories of her late husband in the least. Jim's presence is very much felt in the cozy house where Ingrid and A.J. live (Ingrid has not remarried) in San Diego: Jim's picture, hanging in the front hall, is the first thing you see when you walk in the front door; his gold records on display in a room off the hall, are the second. There are also a number of photos of Jim in the room of thirteen-year-old A.J. who, although he was too young when Jim died to really remember him, "misses having a Jim," says his mother. "But he laughs a lot about him. And there's still lots of people that knew him as a person—not only as a star—who discuss with A.J. how much he's like him."

■　■　■

Ingrid Croce is in the midst of making up a big batch of cherry blintzes in her sunny, flower-filled kitchen. As she transfers the batter from bowl to cookie sheet, she talks about her plans to open up a fast-food blintz store—the first of many, she hopes—in San Diego. Watching Ingrid, who works quickly and efficiently—the blintzes seem to be done in no time—one would think that she's been working in the food business for years. "No," she says, in an interestingly froggy voice (which turns out to be the result of a recent throat operation), "I was in the music business from the time I was fifteen until about a year and a half ago. At fifteen I was singing with these two guys at school in Philadelphia" (Ingrid's hometown, though on this day, dressed in a sleeveless workout tight and sweatpants and looking very fit, Ingrid looks like a native Californian). The only music that Ingrid knew then was show tunes, but somehow her trio ended up entering and winning a folk music contest at Convention Hall in Philadelphia. One of the judges for the contest was a Villanova University sophomore student named Jim Croce. Ingrid and he talked briefly there, and then, a few months later, they ran into each other again at a local radio station. "He was in this group, the Coventry Lads, and as soon as I saw him, it was love at first sight," says Ingrid. "We both went bananas, and that was it. It was not even a question. It was, 'How are we going to do this?' because our backgrounds were Italian Catholic and Jewish. All of the things you think impossible kind of disappear immediately. You don't see them when you're in love. You think everything's going to work out— and it usually does for a period of time until the illusion starts to break through, and all the reality pours in. There wasn't a lot said, because he was kind of shy, and I was real scared because I wanted to look very grown up. I was fifteen and wanted to look maybe twenty-one!"

In any case, Jim offered her some practical advice that day: He told her to forget about singing Gershwin and try rock and roll and folk music instead. "I knew *nothing* about folk music," says Ingrid. "Well, I knew all of three songs,

'Five Hundred Miles,' 'A Cruel War Is Raging,' and maybe 'Lemon Tree.' " But as soon as she met Jim, Ingrid went on a campaign to look more like a folk singer. "I immediately grew my hair and changed my hairstyle to straight bangs and long straight hair." Then she and Jim began to sing together professionally. "And from the time I was fifteen, until he died, we always sang together."

They got married four years later, when Ingrid was nineteen and a sophomore in college. To cover the expenses of the wedding and Ingrid's college education, Jim made an album on his own in 1966. Then, when Ingrid was in her last year of school, they made a folk album together, for which they wrote all the music, for Capitol Records called *Approaching Day*. "Its sales were disappointing. We got no promotion. The bottom line was that we were on the road making about two hundred, three hundred dollars a week that basically covered expenses." For the most part, they performed at college concerts and small clubs. But Ingrid remembers that some club owners weren't too enthusiastic about hiring them. "We were just so straight! The two of us looked so happy together that people said, 'Hey. We want a guy who's going to go out with the girls in the club and a girl who's going to go out with the guys in the club. We don't want a married couple.' We weren't into the game-playing, so that sort of negated our getting certain jobs. We were real down-to-earth. We were not like the kind of people you read about as stars—like the guy bringing back a six-pack of women." One of their stops on the road was a little club in the middle of nowhere in Pennsylvania called the Little Paddock, a place where Jim would continue to play right up to his death. "All the people that he wrote songs about were there," says Ingrid. "It was getting in touch with reality, because you lose the perspective—although Jim's music kept him closer to the people than most people's music does."

When A. J. Croce was born in 1971, Jim and Ingrid

stopped working together professionally. While Ingrid
looked after the baby, "Jim wrote his pieces that finally
made it and probably will be classics forever." After working so closely together for so long, was Ingrid envious when
Jim started to make it on his own? "Never," says Ingrid
decisively. "That was something Jim and I never had. I
don't want to be famous in terms of other people. The price
that you pay for fame is one that I am not willing to pay."

In the last few years of his life, Jim was rarely home,
says Ingrid. "There were periods when Jim was on the road
for three hundred sixty-five days a year. And once he got
on the road, the road trips started to get to him. His personality was very humble, and he had a lot of humility but,
yes, he went through the same road trips that anybody else
goes through. And I say everybody else goes through—because I don't know anyone—I think Dick Clark probably
is the knight in shining armor. He's the only one at this
point, to my knowledge who is really super-straight and
super-nice. I'm not saying the other people aren't nice—
they've all just needed to go through certain experiences to
balance that stardom. It's a heavy trip. You don't ever have
a minute to yourself or a chance to really be with people
and not know why they're with you. I think that his background was such that there must have been certain questions he needed to answer—about other women. About
what it's like to be famous. Yeah, there were problems like
any marriages go through, and in fact the highs were extremely high. The lows were extremely low, but there was
not even a question that we were together.

"I think what happened in the relationship," Ingrid continues, "with Jim and I—and I think it happens to people
who are married to someone who needs to please—the
person that they love becomes the person they feel the most
comfortable with, and therefore they don't have to be as,
quote, 'good' to them as the public. So I became less important as the public became more important. There was
the feeling that he had to please everybody—he felt he even

Ingrid Croce with her son, A.J. The picture in the
background is of her late husband, Jim Croce.

had to please the fans. I don't say the reason that Jim was
with other women or whatever he did on the road was because he had to please the fans, but in a sense, yeah. If
you're used to spending your life pleasing people and the
people that you love aren't around, well, please the ones
you're with. Make them happy, because then they'll
love you."

Jim did call home every day when he was on the road.
"Every day you could hear the frustration in his voice being
on the road and being away from possibly me but mostly
A.J., really wanting to see his son grow up. Even so, he
kept plugging and toiling away on the road, because he
needed to know that he was a success financially. His family always said, 'Jim, you'll never make it in music. Be a
civil-servant worker and get a nice nine-to-five job. Use your
college education.' "

While Jim was on the road, at home Ingrid was going

crazy. " 'Cause I wasn't real happy being alone on a farm in the middle of nowhere until Jim came home. It was not my style. I took care of the baby from eight to eight. Then it was my time, and then I was alone. And Jim was real possessive on his end. He didn't want me with anybody or even near anybody. I think that occurs when you start feeling guilty yourself. You start feeling that other people might be in the same position." But, she adds quickly, "It was never a question—no matter what Jim did—that he loved me. He might have hated me, but he loved me. I might have hated him, but I loved him. And I didn't know him in the sense that I think I know him now, after the fact, and knowing myself better. I guess what happens when most people get married in the music business either after marrying a star, or even before, and having the person you marry, male or female, become a star, is that neither of you have had the chance to build a basis for a relationship—which is difficult in itself."

The last weekend that Jim and Ingrid spent together before he died was, Ingrid thinks, "just about the best weekend we ever spent because he just went through everything he felt. He didn't want to discuss what happened on the road, because it wasn't him. He was planning on producing an album that I was going to do that November—that September he died—we practiced the songs that I was going to do on the album. And there probably would have been a new resurgence of cowriting after he came home."

Was Jim a mentor for Ingrid? "Not really," she answers. "I never felt equal to Jim. I never felt unequal to Jim. We just did it. Music was like making love, making food, doing the things we did well together. It happens to be special because it can be sold as a commodity at a very high price. And that's why this business is so rough. And the most difficult thing for the artist is that you are the art—you are the product and you can't run the product and be the product at the same time. If you are the product,

you really can't take care, you can't protect, you can't be
as cautious as the person who is not the product. So there's
a lot of exploitation—not of the wives any more than the
musicians."

Ingrid speaks from firsthand experience: When Jim died,
all of the royalties from his songs went to the producers, a
situation that Ingrid has been trying to rectify for the last
eleven years. The evidence of her struggle is all neatly stored
away in the wall-to-wall filing cabinets in Ingrid's study.
"My life has been spent trying to untangle the things that
have occurred because of Jim's fame," she says. "When he
died and the money started to come in, he wasn't there to
receive it. It was all tied up in the business and the people
who managed the business. I'm not being paid the royalties now. The same people are getting them as I've been
fighting for ten years. They were supposedly Jim's best
friends. I don't think an artist should go out on the road
and not make a penny, and I felt real responsible for the
money that Jim made. So I just went out and did the liti-
gation—crazy!" Ingrid shakes her head. In the course of
the years, Ingrid says she has gone through "hundreds" of
lawyers. "And there've been probably two or three that I
can say are friends. I'm not quite done with the leeches
and the hangers-on. Anytime there's money, anytime there's
gold, people just go for it, and you're just in the way. It's
a fast life out there, and when everybody's taking and you're
trying to hold on, it's much harder to hold on to things
than it is to go out and get it. I think it's really difficult,
not only for the widows of the music business but for the
widows of anybody in a fast-lane marriage."

With the fast-food-blintz franchise that Ingrid hopes to
start, then, she hopes to "get into a financial position that
is stable for me where other people are not trying to take
what is ours and where I feel secure."

Thirteen-year-old A. J. Croce, who has arrived home
from school for lunch, turns out to have the same rumpled

dark hair and complexion of his father. And, according to his mother, looks were not the only thing he inherited from Jim. "He's got the energy of Jim. He writes music. He's got a lot of the comedy aspect, the same kind of warped humor that Jim had."

But in other ways, A.J. is very different from his father. "He's a lot lighter. And," Ingrid has discovered, "we are able to do things Jim was not able to do, which is really to share our feelings. Jim found it real difficult to express his feelings, and perhaps that's why his songs were so dynamic, because like in 'I Have to Say I Love You in a Song' he could put those feelings into songs instead of having to say it in person. It was real difficult for him to use those words."

*B*ebe Buell

TODD RUNDGREN;
ROD STEWART;
ELVIS COSTELLO;
STIV BATORS

"I used to look at Marianne Faithfull or Anita Pallenberg, and those girls were gorgeous to me when I was a little girl. I used to think, 'Jesus, they are so free, they are so wild-looking. Boy, these must be the girls that make the whole fucking thing tick.'"

*B*ebe Buell is a woman known in music circles for having a weakness for rock stars. At various times, Bebe— a former Ford model and Playboy Playmate—has been linked romantically with Todd Rundgren, Rod Stewart, Elvis Costello, and punk-rocker Stiv Bators of the Dead Boys. Not bad, for someone who wanted to be just like Marianne Faithfull—the quintessential rock and roll girl-friend—when she grew up. "I liked her life," says Bebe. "She was going with a Rolling Stone, who to me were like the coolest guys on earth. So rock and roll and music was something I decided upon very young, as an environment. I liked the way it looked like those people were living— this wonderful freedom, the attitude of no restriction, just being able to travel where you want."

Bebe was seventeen and just starting out as a model and living in a women's residence run by nuns in New York when she was introduced to her first rock star. She was on her way to a play with a friend one evening when he an-nounced that he had to stop by solo-musician and pro-ducer Todd Rundgren's place to drop off some tapes. "I said, 'No way am I sitting down here in the car. I'm com-ing up!' Then, when Todd came to the door, that was that. It was immediate, it was destiny, it was meant to be. So I changed my whole life. I mean, if it wasn't for Todd, I would never have even met any of the rock and roll cir-cle." Some weeks later, Bebe moved in with Todd, al-though by doing so she provoked a lot of people. "I had a very angry mother and a very angry agent and very angry friends who had thought of Bebe as a sweet little virgin from Virginia, who was now not a virgin, living with a rock star and going to Max's Kansas City too often." Todd and Bebe were together for six years, breaking up shortly after the birth of their daughter, Liv, in 1977.

In a short time, Bebe was being squired around town by Rod Stewart. That affair lasted eight months. Next in line was English New Wave star Elvis Costello, who left his wife and son to live with Bebe in London in 1979.

When Elvis decided to go back to his family some months later, Bebe was heartbroken. For consolation she turned to punk-rocker Stiv Bators. In 1980, Bebe quit modeling and moved up to Portland, Maine, where she lives today, alone.

■ ■ ■

Bebe Buell stands at the doorway to her bedroom and looks around. "Most guys think they need to wear a tutu to come in here," she says. One can see why. The predominant color in Bebe's bedroom is pink, and crammed with so many plastic poodles, flamingos, Kewpie dolls, Barbie dolls, stuffed pink panthers and pussycats, toy cars, and heart-shaped pillows that one might think that the room belonged to Bebe's seven-year-old daughter. "Well, we do fight over who plays with what," says Bebe. In her tight black jeans and black sweater, Bebe looks every bit as curvy in person as she does in the *Playboy* and *Oui* pictures of herself on display on the living room wall next to her vinyl record collection.

It's a surprise when Bebe confesses that as a teenager in Norfolk, Virginia, she never went out with boys. "I was terrified of dating," she says. "All the guys at school were just like these animals—you sit down in their car and they just go for it immediately. I just didn't like that. I just thought that sex was something you did when you finally met someone who didn't hit on you like an animal.

"I felt most comfortable in my room with my rock magazines and my Rolling Stones records and my occasional

Dave Clark Five or Monkees record," she continues. "And I really did withdraw into that little room quite a bit."

Back then, Bebe's favorite group was far and away the Rolling Stones—"the band that really changed my life and made me become a preordained rebel." As far as Bebe was concerned, their music was far more enticing than that of the Beatles. "The Beatles to me were always either totally in love or totally after love, which I didn't object to, but the Rolling Stones presented danger and the chance for choice and the quest for something a little bit different, something a little less perfect. And I thought about Mick Jagger as the guy that helps my mind escape school and family pressure."

At age eleven, Bebe and a friend, accompanied by Bebe's mother, went to their first Stones concert at the Virginia Beach Dome. Bebe remembers: "We had our crooked little Marianne Faithfull haircuts and we were ready to go. And my mom let me wear lipstick—it was a big night for me. At the concert, my mom got up to go to the bathroom, and I had my Instamatic camera, and she forbade me to go to the front, 'cause there was a whole line of policemen. But as soon as she went to the bathroom, boy, I charged. And it looked real funny, because nobody was charging. I remember Mick Jagger looking out into the audience and going, 'You really are a quiet lot.' Nobody was screaming. But I ran up and knelt down and I picked up my camera and I went clicko. I have pictures of Brian Jones. To the Stones, it was wonderful that somebody was moving. And so finally this cop came over and grabbed my arm, and it was real intense because he did not move from his position against the stage. He was macho! He tried to move me, and I went, 'No way.' So Keith came over to the edge of the stage and took his foot and pushed the cop in the head with his foot. This got in the newspapers. And they let me stay there. So it took five fucking minutes for the whole place to be up and, 'Yeah, she gets to do it, so do we!' "

Being the obsessed Stones fan that she was, Bebe, naturally enough, became fascinated with their girlfriends. "I used to look at Marianne Faithfull or Anita Pallenberg, and those girls were gorgeous to me when I was a little girl. I used to think, 'Jesus, they are so free, they are so wild-looking. Boy, these must be the girls that the guys write the songs about. These must be the girls that make the whole fucking thing tick.' That was before they called girls groupies. Because rock and roll, when it first started with the Rolling Stones and the Who and the Beatles, the girls they hung around with were these creatures of exception. For some weird reason it was spiritually ordained that these strange unions would come about, and then, girls, like flies, really started to want this too. And so then, like anything, it got cheap on a lot of levels, because girls started hanging around alleyways like cats meowing in fishnets at the boys, becoming like a prostitution ring instead of real muse relationships, which has been a part of music for centuries."

Somehow, Bebe knew that she was going to end up being like these women. "I was very fortunate at a very young age to get a glimpse into my future. Something was letting me know real early. So I had plenty of time to get ready."

So by the time Bebe had graduated from high school and was headed for New York to become a Ford model, she had all her homework done. In the beginning, though, Bebe laid low. She lived in Saint Mary's, a women's residence run by nuns; lugged her portfolio around town; went for test shots; and stuck faithfully to the 1:00 A.M. curfew imposed by Eileen Ford on all of her young models. And then: "I started losing my mind. I said, 'What the fuck—I need some new rock and roll. Where is Mick Jagger?' I started thinking about this place, Max's Kansas City, I kept reading about and how maybe I should go there. So I got all dressed up and I got on the bus and I'd go right down Second Avenue and get off at Irving Place."

From the moment that Bebe stepped inside Max's, she

knew it was her kind of place. She remembers thinking, "Boy, this is great!" "The first night I was there, I met Andy Warhol and people involved in the fashion and entertainment industry. Debbie Harry was a waitress when I first went there. She had brown hair, and I used to think she was so beautiful and I used to say, 'You know, man, this girl—why is she waitressing? She should be a rock star.' And she had charisma, too. She'd go up and dance and she had something about her. She was shy and everything, but she had this little light around her. There was another girl named Dory who was really pretty and I used to feel like maybe I should go dance next to those girls."

Once Bebe discovered Max's, she started to blow her curfew ("And I actually slept through a test for a *Glamour* cover"). When Eileen Ford got word of Bebe's behavior, she called Bebe into her office and bawled her out. "She was pissed off at me no end," recalls Bebe. "She said, 'Man, if you do not cool out, I'm going to have your mother come and take you home. You're running around too much.'"

Bebe had been in New York just three months when she met Todd Rundgren, the former leader of the Nazz, who was now producing albums for bands like Badfinger and Grand Funk Railroad. When Bebe went up to his apartment for the first time, it impressed her as being "such a weird environment. Piano over there and things hanging everywhere. It was sort of cluttered and packed with shoes and clothes and records and instruments and tapes, just amazing. And the most unusual, unique wardrobe, because he wore real English fashions before other American people did."

After Bebe and Todd started dating, Bebe soon started staying in that apartment all night, "like most normal people. Finally, one day, I just didn't go back to Saint Mary's."

As Bebe tells it, living with Todd lived up to her expectations in "every single solitary way. Because I was totally in love with him, and he was one of the smartest people I ever met in my life. One of those kind of people who could take apart a television and put it back together again, or I'd come to him with a broken strap on a shoe and it would be fixed in five minutes. He was also really into having fun. He'd take me places I'd never been. Private parties. He would also take me to acupuncture parties and he would take me to meet a guy that would sit around and talk about the theory of letting water drip in the middle of your head for an hour. He'd take me out to a Hindu or some weird restaurant. I was really exposed to a lot of great, wonderful, different things."

Bebe Buell in her bedroom, Portland, Maine.

Through Todd, Bebe got to meet some of her idols, including singer Patti Smith and—at long last—Mick Jagger. He was just what she thought he would be: "brilliant and articulate and fun and very sane and very in control of his body and his mind." At the same time, she realized that she would never really want to be his girlfriend. "Only because I don't think I could ever share somebody that much. I just am not somebody who can handle constant, constant public persona. You lose touch of yourself."

Life with Todd, however, didn't just consist of going to parties and meeting famous people. Bebe continued to model, appearing in magazines like European *Cosmopolitan*, *Harper's Bazaar*, and *Vogue*, and in 1974, in *Playboy* as a centerfold. According to Bebe, it was Patti Smith who urged her to try out to be a Playmate. "She said, 'Oh, do it. It'd be really daring. Stick it right up those fashion bastards' asses.' " While Bebe was waiting to hear whether she'd made it into the magazine, she met Hugh Hefner. "If anyone is under the illusion that Hugh Hefner makes love to all the girls on the centerfold, that's really a bunch of bullshit. The one time I did meet him, he was playing Monopoly and drinking Pepsi-Cola with a pair of glasses on, and he was sitting there with this gorgeous blonde with the biggest tits I had ever seen in my life. I just said, 'Hello,' and he said, 'Are you going to be a Playmate?' and I said, 'I hope.' And he looked at me like, 'No way.' But he liked my pictures. That's how he picks the girls, from their photographs. He's not a lecherous man."

Bebe was too busy working to always go with Todd on tour, though she made sure she was always by his side in cities like LA, where, according to Bebe, the groupies are "real thick. If you're married to somebody in rock and roll, there are definitely places where you don't let your husband go without you—unless you want him to completely have nights of decadence, because it's just like the way it goes in LA. These women are very loose out there. Women coming up to you, 'Do you want a blow job?' I mean, give me a break, what guy doesn't?" But even with a wife or girlfriend along, the rock star, it seems, is still not entirely safe from the clutches of groupies. "They're crafty. They'll come up to you and go, 'Want us to take you shopping? We know all the great places to go.' If you come into LA for the first time and you don't know your way around, two of them take you shopping and two of them go after the guy. This is where you're talking hard-core groupie here—the girls that really have the science down." Bebe claims that she herself never stooped to those measures. ("I *never* did that shit!") Nor has she ever gone backstage and just stood against the wall like an ornament, just to be with a rock star ("That's being a hooker"). "It's really funny," she says. "Everyone I met involved in music, I've always met them in a situation. I've never met anybody I've ended up with backstage. Not to say I've never met anybody backstage. When you visit somebody, when you do the backstage shuffle, as I call it, yeah, of course you meet tons of people, but you certainly don't date every single person you meet. I'd be fucking crippled if that was the case."

Although Bebe has often been called a groupie in the press, when it comes right down to it, she does not consider herself one. "I consider myself a fan," she says. "But you know," she adds, "I have to admit that I really enjoy musical men. I'm not gonna sit here for one minute and say that I don't."

In her six years with Todd, Bebe admits that she found it very difficult to be monogamous." I was young and I was exposed twenty-four hours a day to some of the most exceptional people," she reasons. "From the age of eighteen onward are big times for people. You make all your mistakes and you definitely become sexually experimental."

Even so, Bebe did experience some conventional yearnings: "I really wanted to get married. And I really wanted to have a baby." As it turned out, only one of her wishes was granted. In 1977, she had Todd's child. Marriage, however, was not in the cards. "Todd and I never wanted the same things at the same time. Then he fell in love with another woman. No other way to put it," she says matter of factly. Bebe considers the period after she broke up with Todd as "total irrational insanity, which included dates with

Rod Stewart, which I can't even believe I did. I would never have dated Rod Stewart if I'd been in my right mind and if I hadn't been in as much pain as I was in from the rejection of getting replaced. But I learned what it's like to be used as a press object in the relationship of knowing that man. Rod Stewart is a dangerous person as far as I'm concerned, if you're a woman. Because even if you go out with him once, it's plastered everywhere, and for some fucking weird reason, he's always used it as a method of getting attention. He gets something from being with anybody who's a little bit in the public eye. It's part of his persona; he's always gone out with women who help attract the press. He likes that. But I think it's really unfair to the girl, because what if you wanted to go out with somebody a couple of times and you didn't want anybody to know, just to feel out the situation, but there's nothing you can do about it. I think he's fucking abused the shit when it comes to using people on that level."

Did Bebe at least like Rod's music? She answers: "Quite frankly, when I was a little girl, I used to like some of the Faces' stuff. I can't lie. Sure I liked his music, but he wasn't that person by then anymore. He was not the Rod Stewart who lived in England anymore. He was a bleached-blond guy that was the victim of a lawsuit [by former girlfriend Britt Ekland] that lived in Los Angeles. He was just a guy, a little jerk. All he wants to do is go out. I don't think Rod had a domestic bone in his body. And I think that's an important part of a guy, that he can relax at home." Not surprisingly, Bebe was not heartbroken when she and Rod parted company after eight months. "If you don't love somebody, what pain?" she says. "The only pain I experienced was that the whole issue was slapped all over the papers, and it made me look like I was at the bottom of the knife, which really wasn't what happened. The only two people who ever really mattered to me were definitely Todd and Elvis [Costello]."

Bebe met New Wave singer/songwriter Elvis Costello at

the Whiskey Club in Los Angeles right after she had seen him in performance at Hollywood High. "I thought the show was wonderful. I talked to him for a while, and then we [that is, Bebe and a girlfriend] left, and that was that. I didn't get to know him too well then. And then I heard from him. He sent the letter to a friend to give to me. Then I wrote him back, and the rest is history. Then it became like a mad phone thing. Months of phone." One thing led to another, and eventually, Bebe and Elvis ended up living together in London for five whole months before he went back to his wife and child. In retrospect Bebe says she doesn't feel any guilt about having had an affair with a married man. "It really depends on the status of the marriage. If the marriage is happy, then the man is being selfish and just having fun, then I don't approve of that at all. For me personally as a woman, I don't believe I should be anybody's extramarital heyday, but I certainly do not feel that way about Elvis."

Although Bebe's affair with Elvis was fairly brief, she says, "The whole thing affected my life very much. A lot of things happened that led up to me having to believe a lot things about myself. Self-growth that I had to really work on. It's like I was really too young, mentally, to possibly realize how much I loved him. It wasn't until way after he went back to England, back to his wife and everything, and after two years of not seeing him and talking to him, it sort of hit me one day like a ton of bricks. And then I realized I really had to start working on stuff like commitment. And as I got older and everything started falling into perspective, I found out I would much rather have married Elvis Costello than Mick Jagger any day."

When Elvis left, Bebe went through another one of her, in her words, "little temporary insanities." She tried to recover from the affair by taking up with punk-rocker Stiv Bators. "Everybody thought we were much more serious than we were. We were really more than anything just real good friends. We sort of loved taking the piss out of every-body. We looked like this modern Sonny and Cher. We hammed it up, we had a real good time. And he thought it was a good way for me to release myself from the pain I was feeling. Because, I mean, everybody knew I loved Elvis and that was that. He is the man I love. Period. Anybody who has gotten involved with me since I've met that man has got to accept that. It is just not going to go away."

One has only to see Bebe's apartment in Maine to take her at her word. On display are large Elvis posters, Elvis buttons, backstage passes to Elvis Costello and the Attrac-tions concerts . . . Standing on Bebe's bedside table, there is a framed picture of Elvis.

After Elvis, Bebe tried living on her own in New York, but the cost of living there proved to be too much for Bebe's income (she had quit modeling). So in 1980 she moved up to Portland, Maine, into the lower half of a modest wood-frame house. "I am a neurotic housewife that has no hus-band," she says. "I clean this house. Go under the bed," she urges. "You could sleep under it! I just enjoy keeping everything really clean and together." (That's for sure: When the photographer moved one of her rocking chairs a couple of inches, Bebe immediately rushed over to put it back in its original position.)

Bebe, as it turns out, has had musical ambitions for her-self all along and has only recently found the courage to act on them. Since she left New York, Bebe has made an EP record called *Cover's Girl*, produced by Rick Derringer, and formed a band called the B-Sides, with whom she has toured several times. Someday, she says, she'd like to do a record with Elvis ("Who wouldn't?"). But for now, while she's waiting for her career to take off, Bebe lives off the money earned from her modeling days and from her oc-casional part-time jobs teaching local high school girls how to apply makeup or working as a hairdresser's assistant. For now, Bebe's daughter, Liv, is living with Bebe's mom in Virginia because, says Bebe, "I need this time very definitely to really consummate what I'm doing. I have to be able to just get on a plane and go to New York when I have to be there for a meeting that's really important. It's like . . . I have no love life so . . . and I have no mom life now, I just sort of have studio life. My twenties to me were my time of experimenting, learning, aching, finding my direction, my profession, what I wanted to do the most. My thirties I'm gonna devote to my artistic tendencies."

Bebe gets up from the living room couch, where she's been sitting, to change her clothes for the photo session. When she returns, she is wearing a Humphrey Bogart T-shirt. She looks down at the shirt and smiles. "They don't make men like this anymore," she says, then changes her mind. "Well, maybe Elvis . . ."

Leslie Meat Loaf

MEAT LOAF

*"Taking care of Meat Loaf is a
full-time kind of thing."*

*M*ention the name Meat Loaf, and people will smile. Then say, "Meat Loaf's wife," and they'll really start to giggle. Somehow, you just don't think of a 250-pound rock star whose image is that of a beer-can-eating, rock-chewing lug who throws women around onstage as someone who would go out and get married. No matter that Meat's *Bat Out of Hell* was one of the biggest-selling LPs of the seventies, or that he is a trained actor with an operatic tenor voice who has appeared in the stage production of *Hair* and the films *The Rocky Horror Picture Show* and *Americathon*. People still say, "Who would marry Meat Loaf?" The answer to that question is Leslie Edmonds, who met Meat in January 1979, when she was working as an assistant studio manager for Albert Grossman (he was the ponytailed manager for Bob Dylan and Janis Joplin) at his recording studio in Woodstock, New York. At the time, neither Meat nor Leslie were looking to get married. Meat had sworn in several interviews that there was no room in his life for a woman. And marriage was obviously not a major priority for Leslie, who had given birth to a daughter, Pearl, in 1975 but had never bothered to marry the father, a musician in Joplin's Full Tilt Boogie Band. However, Leslie says their meeting was "magical and spiritual and real personal. A lightning bolt came down from heaven and said, 'You must marry each other.' " Three weeks later they were married by a ninety-six-year-old priest at Todd Rundgren's home in Woodstock. Pop singer Karla Bonoff sang "Here Comes the Bride."

At home, Meat Loaf (he got his nickname from a high

school football coach—his real name is Marvin Lee Aday, but he's never referred to as anything other than Meat by his wife) is nothing like his onstage image. He coaches three Little League softball teams, helps Pearl (whom he has legally adopted) with her homework, and plays Leggos with his and Leslie's own four-year-old daughter, Amanda, a dead ringer for Meat "with a set of lungs to match," says Leslie.

■ ■ ■

On a cold Saturday in March in Stamford, Connecticut, the entire Meat Loaf family is at home. Upstairs, daughters Pearl and Amanda and their playmate, Chudney, who is Diana Ross's daughter, are singing along to a record given to them by Pearl's godmother, Maria Muldaur. Downstairs, a subdued and streamlined Meat Loaf is sprawled on a leather couch, watching the women's downhill skiing championships on a large-screen television. "He's lost ninety pounds on the Cambridge Diet," says Leslie proudly as she passes around a plate of (no kidding) meat loaf sandwiches. Nevertheless, he still looks large next to fine-boned and delicate Leslie, who might weigh all of one hundred pounds. Leslie and Meat are in the midst of trying to sell their seventeen-room house, and Leslie confesses that she's tired of having to put up with strangers tramping through her home and over the pretty lawn, where she and Meat and the kids like to play croquet in the summer. But what else is to be done? Because of some legal entanglements, Meat's affairs are in a state of bankruptcy, and selling the house, which comes with a natural-formation pool, is an absolute necessity.

The Meat Loaf house has been attracting the inevitable gawkers, who come expecting to see a "rock and roll house with Lucite pianos and eccentric furnishings," says Leslie. Instead, they are treated to the sight of a tastefully furnished home with things like gleaming tea services on display and furniture with sunny floral patterns. Leslie Meat Loaf has put a lot of time into making her house homey, cozy, and traditional, and she has succeeded. It's no surprise, then, when she admits that she's spent much of her life "making homes comfortable and happy places for people." The daughter of a naval officer, Leslie left home in Pennsylvania at age seventeen to take care of a widower's house and four children in Boston. A year or so later, she accompanied a woman friend and her child up to Woodstock for an indefinite stay. This was the year before the Woodstock Festival, and Leslie fell in love with the town. "It was the time of flower children and hippies, and everything was fascinating to me," she remembers. "Everybody was working on the festival, making crafts or trying to put together the food concessions. The Hog Farm people were there, and a lot of the bands had moved to Woodstock to set up. They rented homes and set up housekeeping and rehearsed their bands and just lived there."

Through her boyfriend at the time, Woodstock Festival promoter/producer Michael Lang, Leslie met a lot of the bands and their families. In a short time, she was running a number of their houses. "I knew how to take care of children, and a lot of people needed that," she says. "I was good at that, I worked for the Band and all of their wives, and when they would go on the road and their wives were having babies, I'd move in and we'd wait. If it was time, I'd be the one to drive them to the hospital. I would cook, or I'd keep places clean. I would help entertain. If they wanted to have a big party, I could cook food for fifty people, and set it up and clean it up after, and be watching the kids and be making everything look pretty. I put in gardens for people. I helped Maria Muldaur redecorate because 'Midnight at the Oasis' was a big hit and she was on the road all the time." In short, Leslie was the East Coast equivalent of the groupies that Neil Young used to see when he lived in Topanga County in California and observed,

"There are about eight girls who go around keeping house, cooking food, and making love to everyone. It was beautiful."

By the time the festival rolled around in August 1969, Leslie was well established on the Woodstock scene. Her date for the three-day affair was Jimi Hendrix, whose rendition of "The Star-Spangled Banner" was one of the highlights of the festival. Leslie remembers Jimi as being "really intense. Just being around him, if you touched his skin, you could get high by osmosis. He was like an acid trip. It wasn't just that he took heroin or any particular drug—he just took everything. At that time, people used to throw pills onstage, and little bags of marijuana, and you wouldn't know what was in these pills. He used to have a roadie gather it all up and bring it to his room, and he'd sort through it and take whatever. Another thing that he enjoyed doing would be to take a can of Hawaiian Punch and throw a lot of acid in it and leave it in the refrigerator."

After the festival, Leslie decided to stick around. She ended up living in Woodstock for twelve years. Life was easy then. "All we did was eat organic food and breastfeed," she says. "It was just Woodstock, and you were on a roll. It was a ride that you got on and it took you along from one thing to another to another. And rock and roll was like a religion then. It was something to really believe in." Many of the musicians stayed on as well, and occasionally they would end up at Leslie's house. "I had a house that was just always going," she says. "People were always coming over, and I'd always have a big pot of chili or gumbo. Sometimes you'd wake up on a summer morning and there'd be people sleeping on the couch. You'd look under a pillow and say, 'Oh, look, it's Kristofferson.' Or, 'Oh, look, it's Bobby Neuwirth.' " (Neuwirth was Bob Dylan's road manager as well as being a musician himself.)

In her twenties, Leslie dreamed of becoming a recording

engineer like her brother, Tommy. Instead she had a baby. "I had this incredible biological urge to be a mother. My hormones were screaming at me to have a baby. But of course you have to find a man to do that with. And I did. He was a musician." Leslie and the musician (she won't reveal his name—only the name of his group, the Full Tilt Boogie Band) lived together for seven years, but never married. "He was still married to someone else," says Leslie. "He hadn't seen the woman in thirteen years, but he just never bothered to get a divorce." That relationship fell apart when Pearl was one and a half, and Leslie went to work at Albert Grossman's Bearsville studio, where she had plenty of opportunities to meet musicians. There were periods, though, when she didn't want to have anything to do with them. "It can be very painful," she says. "They're always going on the road and screwing around. I saw a lot of women that had musicians and constantly cried and

Leslie Meat Loaf with her daughters, Pearl and Amanda.

having terrible fights and calling the hotel room and couldn't find their husbands. They went through this hell. I always thought, 'This will never happen to me.' "

What attracted her to Meat Loaf? Answers Leslie very seriously: "He was a very strong man and he had a lot of strong convictions and he knew what he was doing. I found that attractive because I had found myself in a lot of relationships with people who were sort of like wounded puppies. I found myself mothering them. It was almost like I had to fight this kind of neurosis in myself to allow myself to have a healthy relationship."

After her marriage, Leslie went on tour for the first time in her life. She has mixed feelings about going along on the road. On the one hand, she says, "On tour you get to play out a lot of your fantasies. You get to wear silly clothes. If you want to tease your hair out to here and spray it blue, you can do that on the road—whereas if I did that and took my children to school, it wouldn't be very comfortable." On the other hand, Leslie gets "real tired" on tour. But usually she'll go along, mostly because Meat wants her there. "He needs my support and affection," she says. "Taking care of Meat Loaf is a full-time kind of thing. His health needs looking after because he's asthmatic. He's very shy. He's got an operatic tenor voice and he needs to get eight hours of sleep a night, or else his voice isn't going to be what it should be. He needs to eat a certain kind of food. He takes a lot of vitamins. Then there's the laundry." All of these duties were taken care of by road managers and assistants before Meat Loaf was married, says Leslie. "Then when we married, a lot of those people left. 'Cause a wife can replace four or five people."

Although she was indispensable as far as Meat Loaf's needs were concerned on that first tour, Leslie says being "just a wife wasn't as enjoyable, because everybody else had a job, from the road manager to the background singers, and I felt like a fifth wheel." On the second tour, she took it upon herself to be the wardrobe mistress. "We designed the costumes, my sister-in-law and I. That's the creative part of it. Then, when you go on the road, it's just a matter of maintenance and getting the dry cleaning done. I don't want to do all that laundry, but I found it to be better to do something than to do nothing or to be the wife who sits on a folding chair on the sidelines offstage and waits for everyone else."

At home, Leslie's job is "primarily wife, mother, homemaker. That's what I find to be most important right now. Being that is so nebulous now, it's almost got negative connotations. I do feel like a lot of times I've got to defend it. I've had to go through therapy to learn how to relax with it and allow myself to be that and be good at it and know that it's enough. I really wouldn't want to offend any mothers who have to work, but that's what I would like to be—a real good mom."

As for her children, having a father who is a rock star has its ups and downs. When Pearl was in kindergarten, Meat took her class down to the recording studio in two big limousines, with televisions and sodas stocked in the bars. The kids loved it. But, says Leslie, sometimes Pearl is teased by little boys, who make fun of her father's name or the fact that he is heavy. Two years ago, Pearl's grandfather asked her what she wanted for Christmas. "I guess she had had a particularly hard day with one little boy who was being rude about Meat Loaf," says Leslie. "Because she said, 'If I could have anything in the world, it would be that nobody would ever make fun of my daddy's name anymore.' "

In the last few years, the Meat Loafs have had their share of difficulties. Although his records still do well in Europe, Meat has not had a hit record in America since 1977, and on top of that he is being sued by Jim Steinman, the lyricist for the platinum *Bat Out of Hell* album. Leslie says that Meat Loaf is taking everything pretty well, but for her the experience has been devastating. "The thing that I find to be really painful is that when you're really happening and you've got the limousine and a lot of money, you can always pick up the check and buy your girlfriends and their children expensive gifts. Then when suddenly that isn't there, neither are your friends.

"You hear about people talking about you and your problems behind your back—the people who you'd had in your home and who you really trusted with a lot of your personal thoughts. My brother heard this very close friend of mine talking to someone else about, 'I don't know how Leslie and Meat Loaf could possibly go on a holiday now. They're gonna be broke in another year. He's never gonna make another record and he's never gonna sing again.' That can keep you awake at night and it can really send you to a therapist."

Because of their troubles (currently Leslie's favorite song is "Smile, Though Your Heart Is Breaking"), Leslie has kept herself pretty well isolated from everyone but her family. "Right now my best friends are my kids," she says. "I'm afraid of friendships that are not going to be understanding of the situation. Because I don't want to be hurt, and I've been hurt."

Some evenings, after she puts the girls to bed, Leslie goes up to her office and talks to people that she's met through her Apple 2 Plus computer, which connects by telephone into other computers. "It's all typed out," she says, suddenly animated. "You'll type something, and then you hit the bar twice, and that means it's the other person's turn. I've talked to a guy named Will in Lafayette, Louisiana, whose job is flying engineers and oil riggers out into the Gulf by helicopter. And I've talked to another kid who was going to college to be a city planner. It's a good way to make friends—you don't have to see them."

Jo Howard

RON WOOD

"I'm not happy on drugs. You can't function. You can't look after children."

*O*ne evening in London in 1977, model Jo Howard was invited to a party. Her first instinct was not to go: She was newly separated and tired, having moved into a new flat that day. "Then I said, 'Okay, I'll pop in for five minutes,'" remembers Jo. "So I walked in, and this lunatic came up to me and started doing stupid things behind my back. 'Who is this guy?'" she remembers thinking. "I could see a reflection of him in the mirror and I didn't know who he was." He introduced himself as Ronnie Wood, the newest member of the Rolling Stones and former guitarist for the Faces. Ronnie, who was at the time unhappily married, was, it seems, instantly smitten with twenty-two-year-old Jo. For her part, Jo liked him but thought he was a little too cocky and it wouldn't hurt to bring him down a peg or two. So when Ronnie asked her for a date, Jo informed him that she worked as a shopgirl in Woolworth's and that she would meet him outside the store after she got off work on the following day. "He didn't believe me at first, but I convinced him," laughs Jo. "I said, 'It's a job. Don't laugh, 'cause I have a son to support.'" The next day, Jo, who'd forgotten all about her promise, came home from a modeling assignment to find a fuming Ronnie seated in her living room. "He said, 'I have just been sitting outside Woolworth's for two hours asking everybody coming out of the store entrance where Jo Howard is,'" giggles Jo. "Nyah-nyah. It was the best thing I ever did. It really showed him. He was acting so, 'What do you mean, you don't know me?' and, 'Look, I'm on the back of this cover,' I just, 'Oh, you think you're so great?' After that, he wasn't so flash. He got down to normal." Since then, Ronnie and Jo have been virtually inseparable; in their seven years together, they have been apart only two weeks.

They had two children—Leah, born in 1978, and Tyrone, born in 1983—before they finally got around to getting married in 1985. Today the Woods live in New York City with their children and Jo's ten-year-old son, Jamie, from her first marriage.

• • •

Of all the stories that have been written in the last two decades about the personal lives of the Rolling Stones— the epitome of decadence and sophistication—*domesticity* is not a word that crops up very often. So at the Manhattan brownstone belonging to Ronnie Wood and Jo Howard, it comes as a bit of a surprise to find—beyond the piles of music equipment in the hall—a barbecue and a children's plastic swimming pool in the garden, a kitchen as well stocked with food and gadgets as any you'd find in *House and Garden*, and little children absorbed in watching *Mary Poppins* on television. "I'd like everybody to realize that it's not as crazy as they think," says Jo Howard in her lilting English accent, as her year-old son, Tyrone, who appears to have inherited Jo's peaches-and-cream complexion and bright smile, climbs about on her lap. "I do normal things. I do go out shopping every week and shout and scream at the children when they're naughty. We all sit down to dinner together every night. Ronnie is like any other husband—he'll sit down and 'Oh, this isn't cooked properly,' or he'll eat everything at the table."

The chic Upper West Side of New York is a far cry from the little town of Billericay in Essex, England, where Jo Karslake, the daughter of an architectural modelmaker, grew up. As a child, Jo spent most of her time at school staring out the window and dreaming about the day when she could go up to London and become a famous model like Twiggy.

Jo did leave home when she was sixteen for the fashion world in London. Within three months her face was all over the place: on the sides of buses, on TV commercials, and a group of fashion magazines voted her "The Face of '72."

Jo loved the freedom of living and working on her own, but somehow she was persuaded by her anxious parents to move back home and commute to work from there. For a while, Jo accepted the situation—until she met a wheeler-dealer in the clothing business. "He was my first real affair. I really didn't know anything. We got engaged as a way of getting me out of home," says Jo with a mock wail. (Jo's way of telling her story is very colorful: She is vivacious and acts out the role of every person in her tales.) "We went to America on holiday, and I went and got married in Las Vegas. My parents hated him." Jo groans at the memory. She was just eighteen. Two years and one child later, Jo left her husband—not on the best of terms. "He'd say, 'You're going to suffer, young lady,' and he wouldn't give me any money to look after the kid and he wouldn't give me my car back. He wouldn't give me anything at all. So the more he'd say, 'Six months you'll be in the gutter,' the more I worked harder and harder."

For the next couple of years, Jo was scared to really get involved with anyone again—that is, until she met Ronnie. "Love at first sight," says Jo, smiling. "I suppose it's so corny. But all I could think about was this stupid guy."

In spite of her feelings for Ronnie, in the beginning Jo didn't feel very secure about the relationship. They had one romantic month together, and then Ronnie left for New York on business. Jo thought that was the end of that. She remembers thinking, " 'He's not going to call, I know he's not,' " and, " 'He only treated me like a groupie.' " But Ronnie called the day after he got to the States and asked Jo to join him for a long weekend in Paris, where the Stones were about to start work on their *Some Girls* album. They arranged to meet at a deluxe hotel in Paris. Jo recalls, "I thought I'd be cool and get there early evening 'cause he said he was going to be there Friday *afternoon*." She arrived at nine in the evening, with a special weekend round-trip ticket in hand and asked for Mr. Wood's room. To her shock, she was told that there was no Mr. Wood staying at the hotel. Nor had anyone by that name made a reservation. "I thought, 'Shit, what am I going to do? I'm at the most expensive hotel, and there's no reservation, and, oh, the rotten sod—he's treated me just like I expected.' And I thought, 'Well, I have to stay here.' " Jo managed to get a tiny single room. "All evening I sat there because I couldn't get anything to eat because it was so expensive. So I sat there. Eleven o'clock, nothing. Twelve o'clock, nothing." Jo kept badgering the front desk ("They must have thought I was mad") and plotting how she would escape in the morning without paying the bill before finally dropping off to sleep at 3:00 A.M.

The next thing she knew it was 6:00 A.M. and her bedside phone was ringing. "The man at the reception said, 'There's a Mr. Wood downstairs.' I thought, 'Thank God for that!' So he came up, followed by . . . Keith!" Jo giggles. " 'Oh, God. What on earth has he brought *him* along for?' Keith is still in his junkie stage. So he came in, and it's the first time I've ever seen anybody get a needle—whhhhhht—straight into the muscle. Keith said, 'Oh, I needed that.' And it was just so nothing. I thought it was going to be a bit gory, but the way Keith did it, it wasn't," laughs Jo. The boys, Jo discovered, were late getting in because one of the engines on their Concorde jet had stopped in midflight. "They kept going on about Keith's dessert going all the way down the aisle," Jo recalls. "That was all very well, but I was sitting up all night worrying." The three of them talked—for hours, it seemed to Jo. "I'm looking at Ronnie, 'When's Keith going to go?' And Keith's stoned out of his brain, and there's no way it looks like he's going to move. Then Keith fell asleep, and I remem-

ber falling asleep on Ronnie's shoulder and waking up, and
Keith's still there. Being a junkie at the time, he'd fall off
to sleep for a couple of hours and then wake up and he'd
start putting on music. He didn't leave us alone for three
days." By that time Jo was supposed to go home. Somehow Ronnie talked her into staying. "And you know from
that day I got to Paris, I never really went back. He
wouldn't let me go back to England the longer we got to
know each other. So I just rang up the agency and said I
wouldn't be back for a while. I blew all my modeling jobs.
I didn't care. I only had eyes for Ronnie."

At that time in Paris, the cast of characters in the Stones'
entourage seemed to be undergoing an all-around change.
"Mick was with Bianca, but he was having a secret affair
with Jerry at the same time. Bianca was also in Paris, and
all of *that* was insane."

Jo had never gone out with a rock musician before she
met Ronnie, and her ex-husband taunted her about it: " 'Oh,
we're a groupie now, are we? First it's Ronnie and then it's
going to be Mick.' " Nor was she up on the Stones' music
("I did play this one Stones album—can't remember which
one it was—only because it was in this apartment I rented")
or what went on in a recording studio ("I thought they went
into a little room and they were all going to do it once and
put it on the tape recorder and they'd be home in a few
hours"). Jo made up for lost time by spending most of her
days and nights in Paris watching Ronnie and the guys put
together *Some Girls*. "Ronnie wanted me to sit there and
watch him all the time. He used to say, 'Sit and listen and
watch. You'll learn something.' And he was quite true,
'cause, you know, I could never sing in tune before. And
I used to sit there and listen and think, 'What is it that
they like so much about this? What is it they can hear?'
And I have learned to hear all different things. I can pick
up Ronnie's guitar just like that. And I can pick up Keith's."

Jo was five months pregnant with her "love child," Leah,

when the Stones started out on their three-month tour of
the United States in 1978, but that didn't stop her from
going along. "It was great," she says. "It kept my mind off
being pregnant." At her first Stones concert, she burst into
tears when Ronnie walked onstage. "His friends were saying, 'What on earth are you crying about?' I said, 'I can't
believe it. This isn't true. How can I be going out with
that? All those people screaming and shouting, and that's
just Ronnie. He's a normal guy and he still can't find his
socks, and there he is onstage."

Jo Howard and Ron Wood with their children:
Leah (left), Tyrone (foreground), and Jamie (back).

In the beginning, Jo used to watch the concerts like a
"good girl" from the front row, but as time went on, she
got more adventurous. "I'd get the run of the place, so I'd
go underneath the stage and come up and watch right in
front of the guards. Once I climbed up the scaffolding and

watched it from there." As the weeks on tour went by, Jo remembers that there were times when Ronnie was so tired that he didn't think he could drag himself onto the stage. "He's just staggering around. But then as soon as the curtain opens and everybody screams, there's lots of adrenaline and lots of energy." After the show Ronnie, says Jo, is wound up like a little kid. " 'Did you see that bit there?' he'll say. He's got so much adrenaline, and then you can't fall asleep."

On the road, Jo makes herself useful by packing, unpacking, and sorting Ronnie's clothes, doing his makeup, and making sure that he gets up on time. In return, she gets a crash course in seeing the world. So far, the only place she's been that she really hasn't liked is St. Paul, Minnesota, and that's because a crowd of five thousand people there made a rush for the Stones and their entourage when they attempted to go see Peter Tosh in concert. Jo shudders at the memory. "They were just hammering on the car. I couldn't breathe and I got really frightened. And there were people crawling on top of people. And there was this chick saying, 'Don't! Get off me!' to the security guard. 'Get off me! I'm with him!' And I turned around and went, 'Oh no, you're not!' We got out and got into Peter Tosh's bus, and the kids started climbing the bus and rocking it. But in the end we got out all right."

Jo had her approach to the groupie problem all worked out before she went on tour. "I decided the best way to handle it is to become friends with them," she laughs. "So I'd sit there and I'd talk to all these groupies so they'd think, 'Oh, Jo is so nice.' 'Cause what they want to happen is for you to get upset with your old man 'cause he's sitting talking to this chick for ages and ages and then you're going to have a big argument. They'll step right in then. So the best thing to do is not to get upset."

She was not quite as prepared when it came to dealing with the rest of the Rolling Stones, however. "You've got to be strong to cope," she says. "For the first few years I was with Ronnie, the rest of the Stones, especially Keith and Mick, they would put me through their little tests all the time—just to see what sort of person I was—if I really loved Ronnie or what. Mick would come up and say, 'C'mon, let's go!' I'd go, 'Fuck off, Mick. You should be so lucky!' He was always, always going on at me, and Keith would do it in another sort of way—he'd come up with questions that had double meanings."

According to Jo, Mick can be a bit antagonizing at times. "He'll say, 'This is the boys' and 'Woodie, do you remember when you and I used to take those girls out?' Oh, he does those things. He still does it today. I say, 'Look, Mick. I've heard all these stories before. Try making up something new.' " Jo shakes her head. "I don't know about Mick. He's not happy with himself somewhere in there. That's why he does those little things like that to me. That's why he came out in Mexico and bit me so hard on my shoulder. I had a real bruise there. 'Now Woodie's away—oooooohhh wow!' He pushed me on the bed, and he bit me really hard, and I hit him so hard. I went and told Ronnie, and Keith said, 'Well, after all these years, you should kick him in the bullocks.' "

Jo has nothing but praise for the other Rolling Stones. "Keith's like a big brother, and I get on very well with him. Bill's great, and Charlie's wonderful as well. He's got a great sense of humor—real dry." And, she concedes, "Even Mick can be really great. One time on the first tour I broke down and cried. Ronnie was really horrible to me and he was in the wrong, and he was in the wrong in front of the other guys. I can't remember what it was about, but I was really upset. And afterward Mick came to the room and he said, 'C'mon, Jo. I want to have a word with you,' in front of Ronnie. And he took me into the bathroom and he sat on the bath and he said, 'Look, you've only broken down once on this tour. I've cried three times, broke down three times.

You're really doing great.' And he was really nice. It was the normal Mick there. He can be a really nice guy. It's a shame he isn't like it all the time."

Ask Jo whether she thinks the Stones are chauvinistic toward women (as they have been accused of being in songs like "Under My Thumb"), and she answers with a firm no. "Maybe the odd line might come from Mick. Keith's certainly not a woman-hater. He's sending Patti flowers all the time now. Ronnie was good like that when I was pregnant too. He'd go and get me cups of tea in the middle of the night. He's really good like that. Every time I wanted to go upstairs, especially when I got really big, he'd have to come push me up."

As Jo tells it, the amount of drugs the Stones do these days is minimal. "Even Keith hardly does anything. He'll smoke his joints, but that's about it." But it was a different story a few years ago. "Keith was shooting up all the time with his junk. There were lots of people around who thought to be friends of Keith, they had to shoot up, too. It was horrible. They'd get themselves completely out of it and they'd go over the top and they'd just fall by the wayside, and off Keith would go." Jo will never forget the day that Keith decided to give up heroin. "He turned around to Ronnie, and tears were in his eyes, and he said, 'I'm stopping. That's it. Never again.' You knew that he was really serious. You could see it in his face. And he did stop and he's never been on it again. Keith's a very strong person."

Jo herself went through a "little stage" of experimenting with drugs when she first hooked up with Ronnie and the Stones. "It was around, and I did it. Though I never did anything like put a needle in my arm, ever. I couldn't, and Ronnie couldn't, either." (Although Jo doesn't mention it, it has been reported that Ronnie was sent to a detox center in England for a cocaine addiction.)

It was when Jo was in what she describes as her "All

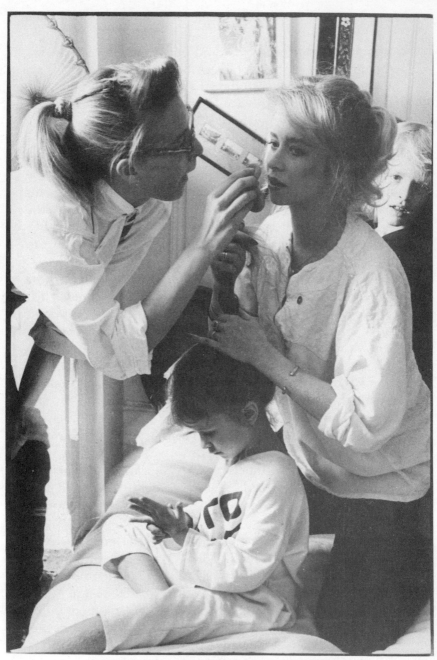

A makeup artist prepares Jo Howard for a photo session. With daughter, Leah (center), and son Jamie.

right, I'll try some of this" stage that she and Ronnie were arrested in Sint Maarten in 1980 for possession of 250 grams of cocaine. She is perfectly willing to talk about the experience and, indeed, makes a good story out of it: "We met these guys who said they've got loads of cocaine. They came out to our house with loads of it and stayed all night and then they asked to borrow our car. What we didn't know is that they had hung a sock in a tree in our garden with 250 grams in it. We were in the house—we had no idea." An observant neighbor had seen them do it, though, and had taken down the number of the car plates, which were, of course, registered in Ronnie's name." Jo was upstairs tidying when the plainclothes policemen arrived. ("I said, 'Oh, not another complaint about the music.' ") Needless to say, the cocaine was discovered, and Ronnie and Jo were taken away to the local prison, leaving their nanny in charge of the children and making the phone calls to lawyers in America.

Ultimately, Ronnie and Jo were charged with trafficking in opium and were locked up for six days. Jo shudders. "If I hadn't stayed up all the night before, I would not have been able to sleep, because it was a stone block. No pillow. No blanket. And a bucket on the floor in the corner." After one night in that cell, she was transferred to another jail across the road. "That's when I first saw Ronnie. Five o'clock every morning he'd go to the shower." Under these circumstances, Jo was beginning to feel a bit nervous. "I was the only white chick there. All these black guys crowded around my cell—it was about twelve guys strung around—and I thought, 'I'm going to be raped in here.' Then this one guy said, 'Hey! You know Ronnie Wood?' " Jo puts on a timid voice. "I said yes. He said, 'Do you know Keith Richards?' I said yes. He said, 'Well, I was with him on the '75 tour!' He was great. He used to pass messages to Ronnie on a stick over the bars. It was all sort of underground prison."

After six days in jail, Ronnie and Jo were released. They got off without even a fine—"There was obviously something very political going on down there," Jo thinks. In any case, Jo claims that that little incident straightened her out. "I certainly wasn't willing to try anything again. And anyway, I'm not happy on drugs. You can't function. You can't look after children." As for Ronnie, well, Jo has a theory that "A lot of musicians get into drugs when they've got nothing else to do with their time. So that's why I keep Ronnie busy all the time. He's been doing lots of painting. Otherwise it would be terrible. He'd be a pain in the neck."

During the interview, Jo's towheaded son, Jamie, keeps poking his head in at the door to the dining room where Jo sits, making a pleasant pest out of himself, like any normal ten-year-old. Recently, Jamie started at a private school in Manhattan. "When I went to the interview for the school, he said, 'Whatever you do, Mom, don't tell them who my dad is. I don't want anybody to know.' So I told the teacher that, and I said this is the way he wants to cope with it. Dad was not allowed to pick him up or take him to school or anything, and then once he got to know his friends and he came home one day and he said is it all right if his friend comes over and spends the night. And this very smart-looking kid comes over, very grown-up. That way he found out who his friends were, and then he let them know who his dad was. I was really quite proud of him."

During her first few years with Ronnie, Jo never considered going back to modeling because, as she puts it, "It's enough having one star in the family." But recently she appeared as an extra in the film *9½ Weeks* and enjoyed the experience so much that she's going to enroll in a drama school. "Now's the time to do it," she says. "I've got my babies and I'm secure with Ronnie. If the drama school doesn't work out, at least I know and I can't turn around in ten years and say, 'If only I'd done this.' My children are going to grow up, and if I look after them all the time now, when they're grown up and left home, I'm going to turn around and say, 'Well, what am I going to do now?' I should have done this when they were younger. They're gonna love me just the same."

When her paycheck arrived for her extra work—her first in seven years—Jo was surprised at how excited she was. "I'm keeping it," she says. "There's nothing like making your own bit of money. I still don't like turning around and saying, 'Ronnie, can I have some money for a new dress?' "

These days, Jo says she's a little more relaxed than she used to be about allowing Ronnie to go on trips without her. Recently, he went down to Jamaica by himself to spend a week with Keith. "One of the reasons I let him go on his own anyway—'cause I could have kicked up a fuss—was 'cause I wanted to see if I was all right on my own as well. 'Cause after a while I started feeling all I ever do is go when he goes. I was fine. I went out to have a massage and I had friends over. It was good for me because I saw that I had friends who would come over to see me even though Ronnie wasn't there. Ronnie rang up one night and he said, 'Well, who's there?' I said, 'Tony's here and Matt Dillon.' 'Matt Dillon??????!!!' I said, 'Yeah, he just popped by to say hello. He brought over *Rumble Fish* for me to watch and off they went!' He sort of moaned and groaned, and as soon as he got back, he made sure Matt Dillon came over!" She giggles.

At this point, Ronnie, having just woken from a nap, enters the dining room where Jo is sitting, in search of cigarettes. With his spindly legs, he doesn't walk so much as he teeters. "Everything all right, luv?" he says, a trifle anxiously. Then they exchange a kiss, and he wanders out again. Their relationship, says Jo, is monogamous. If it weren't, she says, she wouldn't put up with it for one minute. "I'd have to go. To trust in him is so important, and if ever anything happened, I'd just be furious. Anyway, if he loves me and we get on great, then there shouldn't be any reason for him to want anybody else. You have to be happy with what you've got because you know the grass always looks greener on the other side. And it's not really much better out there anyway."

■ ■ ■

All in all, during that interview, Jo came across as friendly, sensible, down-to-earth—the picture of normalcy. Then, two months later, during an evening photo session, Jo was bafflingly an entirely different person. While Ronnie and his friends were boisterously engrossed in watching a Stones video, *Too Much Blood,* Jo was ensconced in the bathroom with the $100-a-night makeup artist and a hairstylist she'd hired for the photo session, acting every inch the star: haughty, cool, remote. And instead of talking to the photographer directly, she'd summon Ronnie's business consultant and gave him the directions to give to the photographer. Perhaps she was just nervous, but the personality change was indeed most perplexing and made one, I'm sorry to say, feel very uneasy.

Carlene Carter

NICK LOWE

*"I haven't been an angel, and
Nick knows it. The thing is, you
cannot live the way we do and
not be tempted."*

*H*ere is a rock marriage in which both partners have their own successful singing/songwriting careers. Carlene Carter, twenty-nine, daughter of country singer June Carter and stepdaughter of Johnny Cash, has written songs for Emmylou Harris, the Doobie Brothers, and the Go-Go's and has herself recorded four rock albums. Carlene's British husband, Nick Lowe (Carlene's third husband), was with the group Rockpile from 1979–1981 and has since gone on to have his own solo singing career and to produce albums for Elvis Costello and for his wife, to name just two.

For Carlene, Nick is the only one of her husbands who has not been threatened by her own musical career. "He's the first guy I've met that felt the same way as me: Why can't we both do it?"

Which is not to say that Carlene and Nick have not had their share of ups and downs in their five-year marriage. In the last year, they have broken up three times, but were back together at the time of the interview in 1984. For the time being at least, Carlene and Nick live in London with Carlene's thirteen-year-old daughter, Tiffany, from her first marriage.

■ ■ ■

Blond hair flying, Carlene Carter bounces into her publicist's office with a great big smile on her face and heads straight for the fridge. "Ah'm dyin' for a beer!" she says in a broad Southern drawl that somehow manages to sound both alien and right at home in the London setting.

Carlene Carter appears to be in a remarkably good mood

for someone whose marriage is admittedly rocky. But then, Carlene's career, which hadn't been going so well in the last couple of years, has recently taken a definite turn for the better: She is appearing on London's West End in a leading role in the musical *Pump Boys and Dinettes*, which has just been nominated for a couple of awards. After being on the road and playing in different towns every night, playing on the same stage night after night is a big change for Carlene. But she likes it—after all, she says, "You never know who's going to be in the audience!" Carlene makes no bones about the fact that she wants to make it really big. "I wanna be a mega-star!" she says. "I wanna be enormous! I wanna be in everything!" Carlene's dream is to do what Dolly Parton did in *9 to 5*—"When it starts out you hear her singing, and she wrote the song. I want to write the title track, I want to do all the music, star in it, and I want to be a huge success!"

That Carlene should have chosen to pursue a career in music seems almost inevitable, considering her background. Her grandmother, Maybelle Carter; her mother, June Carter; and all sorts of cousins and aunts belonged to the legendary country music singing group, the Carter Family. As a little girl, Carlene got to go on the road with the Carter Family, traveling in the back of a Lincoln or a Cadillac. "I could fall asleep anyplace, in any position. I know it sounds like something out of a Buddy Holly film, but when I was a kid, my aunt played an upright bass and I used to sleep in the bass case in the dressing room."

Carlene was all of four when she first went out onstage. "My mom used to sit me on the side of the stage in a chair and she'd say, 'Now stay here,'" Carlene recalls. "She could keep an eye on me and still do the show. One day she turned around, and I was standing on the stage dancing. And I walked to my mom and I said I want to talk on that and pointed at the microphone. She said, 'What do you want to say?' I said, 'My Charlie-dog had puppies. . . .'"

When Carlene got to be a little older, grandmother
Maybelle taught her to play the guitar. Then Carlene took
piano lessons, because she had made up her mind to be a
singer and a songwriter. Her mother, June, was encouraging but said she should first get a college education. So
Carlene bypassed eleventh and twelfth grades and, at age
fifteen, enrolled as a music major at Belmont College in
Nashville. At that point in her life Carlene was, it seems,
in a hurry to do *everything:* The year before she'd gone and
gotten married and had a baby girl. Somehow, Carlene
managed to handle being a college student, wife, and
mother. "It was real hard," says Carlene. "But I was young
and, I tell you, I had bounds of energy."

Carlene's first husband was in college too, and both he
and Carlene held down part-time jobs—she in her parents'
music-publishing company and he in a supermarket, sack-
ing groceries. "Because we were living the same kind of
life actually kept us together as long as it did," says Carlene. "The reason why we split up was basically because I
was fucking sixteen years old. I'd never dated anyone else."

After the divorce, Carlene got a job in a music shop selling sheet music and demonstrating pianos to "people who
didn't know how to play but wanted to buy a piano for
their living room." In her spare time, she was writing songs.
Then she fell in love again, with a songwriter. "He was
very handsome," she recalls. Then Carlene became a teen-
age bride for the second time. That marriage lasted "four
years—that was pretty good!" she jokes. "He was a great
guy, but we just couldn't live together." Apparently the
troubles began when he started to get competitive with
Carlene over their respective careers. For her part, Carlene
swears that she had no intention of competing with him.
"I was the little homemaker and wanting *him* to do good.
But he never hardly worked, because he thought he should
stay home and write songs." So Carlene went to work to
earn some money for the household and continued to write

songs. "Then I got fed up. I mean, I got pregnant about a year after we were married and I was working and he wasn't doing anything. Basically, he was sitting at home and getting drunk a lot. I just snapped one day and I said, 'Look, I'm going to support me and my kids, and you go get a job. If you want to stay home, fine, but I ain't gonna give you nothing anymore."

"He wanted us to do it together, you see," she continues. "He wanted us to be the little Johnny and June. And I wasn't cut out for it too much." It was at that point that Carlene decided that she wanted to make it on her *own*, not as part of a duo. "I love working with people. But I think it ends up splitting relationships eventually. Look at the Everly Brothers. It's taken them so long to get back together."

Carlene's first big career break came when a song that she had cowritten with a woman named Suzanna Clark, "Easy From Now On," was recorded by Emmylou Harris. Carlene was ecstatic. Her husband, to put it mildly, was not. Carlene explains: "The thing was, when I got a song cut, he hadn't really had anything cut, and he started getting kind of, 'You're the little lady—you stay at home.' I just said, 'Fuck you, I'm working my tail off here. If I can work, go to school, have kids, and write songs, how come you can't?' "

The rift between them widened when both he and Carlene were scheduled to play three of their songs in front of Nashville businessmen at a local event called Songwriters Night. At the last minute, he got cold feet, but that wasn't stopping Carlene from getting out there and performing. "I said, 'Well, if you don't feel like singing, just come and watch me do mine.' He said, 'You can't do it.' I said, 'Why not?' Anyway, I just got in my car and left him with the kids and went and did it, and he threw rocks at me while I was going out the driveway. That's how mature he was then!"

That was not the worst of it. Right about the time of the rock-throwing incident, Emmylou's managers and Warner Brothers approached Carlene with a record deal. "My husband said, 'If you do that, it's over.' He was so scared that I would do better than him. And the whole male ego thing . . . After that, it was pretty much downhill."

After their split-up, her husband married Carlene's sister, Cindy (*that* lasted nine months), and Carlene, who'd gone out with only two men in her life, went, in her words, "completely mad." But she was cautious too. "You know how you do those little things to keep yourself from getting in trouble again? I went out and bought myself a little tiny chain ring to put around my finger to remind me every time I thought about slipping a ring on there why I didn't ever want to get married again. Little did I know I'd meet Lowe, so . . ." She laughs.

Carlene met Nick in 1977, at a time when she was riding high in her career. She had just signed her first record contract with Warner Brothers. "I was on a magic carpet. They whisked me over here, and it was limos and the whole bit. I came here to do my album with Dave Edmunds. Dave talked Nick into coming to play. Nick didn't want to come sit in on some bird singer, but he came and played bass. It was funny. I looked at him from behind. He turned around and he was really cute. I just touched his hair and stuff and I said, 'Ooooh, you're a cutie, aren't you?' I just . . . really sparks at first. It's dwindled into cinders now, but . . ." Carlene laughs, in spite of herself.

Nick was not without problems; he drank heavily (he's since quit), but at least he didn't get so darn competitive with Carlene. Says Carlene, "Nick was the first man I met who wasn't threatened at all by me. He was successful when I met him. So I think that helped. Actually," she muses, "I don't think it would bother Nick if I was an enormous star and he wasn't. I don't think it would affect him the way it affected Jack or most men. 'Cause Nick just does his thing, goes along, and has a nice day. He does the best he can and he's a brilliant songwriter."

Right from the start Nick and Carlene lived together well. Nick himself had never been married nor really lived with anyone, though he'd had plenty of girlfriends. "But he always said I was the first girlfriend he'd ever had that didn't make him talk to her in the morning when she woke up. It was funny, but when we were first together, he used to wake up and the first thing he'd say was, 'Don't talk to me.' And I understood it wasn't like he didn't like me or something. He just felt like shit."

There was one geographical problem, however. Carlene's base was in Los Angeles, Nick's in London. In one year Carlene made seventeen roundtrips between LA and London. "I had permanent jet lag. I stopped having my periods. I was like an airline stewardess and I wasn't doing anything. I finally said, 'Look, we have to make a move here.' I wanted to live together, and he wanted to get married. He wanted to do the right thing, you see. Because he's actually very old-fashioned in a good kind of way. He's an RAF brat and he's lived all over the world and his parents are very straight."

So they got married in August 1979, at Carlene's house in Los Angeles, right at the end of the Rockpile tour. June Carter and Johnny Cash didn't make it—"It's just not exactly new to them to see me getting married," jokes Carlene. "Still, it was a fantastic wedding. Billy Bremner, who was the guitarist from Rockpile, was my maid of honor. And Jake Riviera [Nick's manager] videoed our wedding and used it in the video *Cruel to Be Kind*."

Before Carlene was ever married, her mom gave her some advice about marriages in the music business that would prove to come in mighty handy for Carlene: "She said, 'You've got to always remember that when you're out on the road, everyone is telling you you're fantastic. Then you go home and you've got to be normal again. It's really hard to adjust, and you usually get the blues real bad. You get depressed because you come home after all this adrenaline's been going and the one you love isn't going, "Yeah" [Carlene applauds] all the time. And they shouldn't, because you have to come back to normal.' That's where I always try and remember that when he comes home, not to expect him to be normal."

After they were married, Nick produced two albums for Carlene. "The first one was great. The second was really fun, and I liked it. But it was very live and drugged." Carlene's laugh is down and dirty. "It was a filthy album! There were a lot of rude songs on it about fucking and things. I was foulmouthed, and it had lots of innuendos that pointed toward no radio play."

After that album was finished, Carlene and Nick stopped working together. "I wanted him to work with me again, because the best times I used to have with Nick is when we wrote songs together. But we've had some real ups and downs this year. Since we stopped working together, we've grown apart in some ways, and in other ways we've gotten closer."

Since they've been married, both Carlene and Nick have been on the road a lot—one year Nick was gone eight months on the road. The separations, says Carlene, do not help their marriage one bit. "It was like we were living two completely separate lives. It was really hard."

When asked about Nick's conduct on the road, Carlene is unusually candid in her answer. "He's a rat," she says flatly. "One time he told me what he had been doing on the road and he kept saying, 'Come on, Cal, tell me what you've been doing.' " How did she handle that? "I used to beat the shit out of him," she says. "I was so frustrated with hearing about it. I'm incredibly jealous that he's learned if he does do anything, he makes sure it's nobody I know. Because girls love to tell on each other."

If just hearing about her husband's behavior upsets her, imagine how Carlene must have felt when she discovered Nick with another woman before they were married. Carlene's words come out in a tumble as she tells the story: "Nick had forgotten that he had asked me to come pick him up at this hotel. I got there, and this girl was sitting on his lap, and I knocked on the window and I was dying inside, and he turned around and I went [Carlene makes a thumb's-up sign] like that, and he came out, and I said, 'Get her out of there now!' and he said, 'Right.' He was scared. I made him cry he was so scared. So she left, and he cried, and then we got married," she finishes triumphantly.

If Nick is a "rat" on the road, then Carlene is, by her own admission, "the only other rat that's as big a rat as he is. I haven't been an angel, and Nick knows it. The thing is, you cannot live the way we do and not be tempted. What are you going to do when your old man's away for eight months and you work with somebody or meet somebody that you really like? And you feel it happening? And when the feeling's mutual, it's really hard to keep from getting in trouble. It's really scary, but there's nothing you can do about human beings, and if you don't have your mate there, you start looking around. Temptation's just around the corner all the time."

When asked about the current state of her marriage, Carlene sounds a little confused in her reply. "Nick and I broke up for a while. He went on the road and he said he was going to leave, so for the first time ever I said I was going to date people. Then I got a crush on a couple of people, and then Nick did call me a week before he came home and said he loved me again so . . . I don't know. Me and him might be getting a divorce, we might be completely broke up and me be married to somebody else by the time this book comes out. I'd hate it if we broke up, but if we did, I'll be glad we had as good a time as we have. I *think* I could be old with him, but I just think everything is so transient these days." There is a long pause. Then Carlene says, "I definitely won't get married again. No way!" In spite of what she says, though, one gets the feeling that Carlene may just have to get out and buy herself another chain ring.

Vera Ramone

DEE DEE RAMONE

*"I thought he was just the
sweetest, quietest, little thing. I
didn't know he was stoned all
the time."*

*I*n 1977 Vera Boldis was by day a receptionist in an office in New York City's garment district, commuting to her job each day from Queens where she lived with her family. By night, she was a regular at Max's Kansas City, one of the city's most popular music clubs in the seventies. All of the innovative bands played there; Vera can't count the times she saw Talking Heads, Blondie, Television, and the Ramones at Max's. Out of all the groups, Vera especially liked the Ramones—four punks from Forest Hills who wore leather jackets and ripped jeans and played rapid-fire, minimalist songs like "Teenage Lobotomy" and "I Wanna Be Sedated."

One evening in December 1977, Vera was standing upstairs at the bar at Max's when she found herself side-by-side with Dee Dee Ramone (who is definitely considered the cutest Ramone by female fans). It turned out that both Vera and Dee Dee were ordering the same drink, a blackberry brandy. "Which is kind of strange," remarks Vera now. "Because nobody else there was drinking that but us." Then Dee Dee turned to Vera and said, "I'm Dee Dee Ramone." "I just looked at him and said, 'Oh, hello,' " remembers Vera. "And he kept repeating it. Maybe he didn't think I caught on 'cause I didn't have much of a reaction. I knew, but I didn't want him to think I was impressed. Then when I didn't fall all over him, he had to take another step. So, after he namedropped a little and it didn't stir up anything for him, then it was, 'Well, do you come here often?' " Somehow Dee Dee must have struck a spark of interest within Vera somewhere, because that same evening, Vera, Dee Dee, and Vera's sister ended up going club-hopping. Nine months later, to the day, Vera and Dee Dee were married in a most unpunklike traditional church wedding, complete with several bridesmaids in yards of chiffon and a soloist who sang "Ava Maria" from the church balcony. In 1984 Dee Dee and Vera celebrated their sixth wedding anniversary.

■ ■ ■

Whitestone, Queens, does not immediately come to mind as the sort of place where one would think a fairly successful rock star like Dee Dee Ramone would choose to live. TriBeCa, yes. The East Village, possibly. But Whitestone? With its two- and three-family red-brick homes, tree-lined streets, and sprinklers on every lawn, Whitestone is definitely suburban. Yet Dee Dee and Vera Ramone have lived here, in the lower half of a two-family house, since they were married six years ago, and they love it. In turn, their working-class neighbors are thrilled to have a member of a famous rock band living in their midst. "They give you stuff for free," says Dee Dee Ramone proudly. He is slouched on a couch in their small but immaculate living room area and jiggling his feet rather nervously up and down on the top of a glass coffee table. "When we go to the movies, we don't have to pay. And sometimes you go the dry cleaners and you try to pay the bill and they say, 'Ah, forget it.' "

Dee Dee is dressed almost in full Ramone regalia—tight T-shirt, faded Levi's (though on this particular day in July it's too hot even for a Ramone to wear a leather jacket). Vera, by comparison, sitting erect and composed next to him, looks quite dressed up in her black sleeveless jump-suit and huge, dangling feather earrings and an assortment of clunky silver bracelets and rings and quite a lot of eye makeup. Vera says that she's always liked to dress a little wild, even at Catholic school, where she had to wear a uniform. "Everybody had to wear a uniform with the knee-highs and the little berets and the little bow ties," she says. "I had on those little shoes that were out at the time—those Merseyboats. They were really cool-looking, but they didn't look good with knee socks, so I had to wear stockings with them. They sent me home at lunchtime, and I had to come back with the knee socks and the regulation loafers. And I remember one time a nun took me into the hall and washed the makeup off my face. And my hair was teased, so she put my head under the sink."

After high school, Vera tried Queensborough Community College, but dropped out to take a job as a gal Friday in an office in New York. "It was a regular nine-to-five job, but I used to go out at least four or five nights a week and go out till five in the morning and then get up and go to work at six." After checking out practically all the clubs around town, after a while, the only place Vera would go was Max's. Because she was there so often, she thought of herself as "more than an audience. I wasn't just a weekend person that would stroll in. You'd kind of get to know everybody after a while."

Vera had seen Dee Dee around at Max's before, so when they finally did start talking that evening in December, it wasn't like they were total strangers. But even though they hit it off that night and he took Vera's number, it was a while before Vera heard from him again. "He was leaving in a couple of days to go to England for a month and he didn't call me before he left. I said, 'Oh, well, another one bites the dust.' And then I came home one night, and my mother said to me, 'You had a call from England. A Dee Dee called you.' I was like, 'Oh, really?' And then he called back and said he lost my number and that he was having some troubles where he was living before he left." The "troubles," Vera was later to discover, had to do with the girl that Dee Dee was living with at the time. "He got thrown out," laughs Vera heartily.

Vera and Dee Dee Ramone at home in Queens.

When Dee Dee got back from England, they started to date regularly. "I thought he was just the sweetest, quietest little thing," says Vera. "I didn't know he was stoned all the time." Dee Dee, it seems, had started snorting heroin at fifteen, when he was still just Doug Colvin and packing bags in a Forest Hills supermarket. By the time he met Vera, he'd been doing heroin for ten years. Apparently he was so good at hiding his habit that it took Vera a while to figure out what he was up to. "Sometimes I thought I knew, and he would bullshit his way out of it. I'd ask him, 'What'd you take?' He used to take a lot of pills, so I thought that he had just taken some pills and that he was just mellowed out. I don't think I ever really wanted to believe that he was doing hard drugs. And then when I realized how serious the problem was, we were probably married two years. That just crushed me, you know? I thought that if we lived out here, it would be harder for him to go cop. Things were pretty crazy with

us. It wasn't all roses. I was downright miserable for a
while. I didn't know where my marriage was going. I'd say,
'Is this what I want out of life? Isn't this crazy?' I've been
brought up by a strict Catholic family and I've always had
it in my mind to get married and have a family someday
and have a nice house—all those little things that come along
with having a nice life. And it wasn't working out like that.
It was sort of a disaster. Everything he did affected our
lives, and it got to the point where we had to do something about it, because I didn't see it going anywhere. I
honestly believed that he would be dead right now. He's
overdosed, and it's the awfullest feeling. I never want to
go through that again."

Once it got so bad that Vera left Dee Dee for two days.
"I came home and found him lying on the floor. I felt like,
'God, I love you so much. How could you do this to me?' "

Then, one day, out of the blue, Dee Dee picked up the
phone and dialed the number of Odyssey House, a treatment center for drug addicts in New York. That was in
1981. "And he's been going ever since," says Vera with
pride. In addition, she confesses, Dee Dee takes the train
into Manhattan every day to see a psychiatrist.

Still, says Vera, with their life-style, Dee Dee has to be
continuously careful. "This business makes it a lot harder
for him to be straight, because people come up to you, and
a lot of the Ramones' songs are funny, like 'I Wanna Be
Sedated,' they think they're being your friends by giving
you drugs, whether it's a toot of coke or pills or whatever
they had. They think that's the cool thing to do." To Vera,
drugs are anything but cool. "I think they're old-fashioned. The eighties are here, and people should really get
with it. I think drugs are really a bore and I think drugs
are for losers. Anybody that really knows where it's at, they
don't want to be around people who are doing drugs."

The Ramones are on the road for a few months out of
each year. Vera, armed with a duffelbag full of books,

usually accompanies them. "We travel together because we
need each other. This is what works best for us, because
we both get lonely, and if you have long separations, it's
not good for any marriage." And anyway, Vera has a good
time on the road. "You get invited to all the best parties,"
she says. "I've met David Bowie, Chrissie Hynde . . ."
She has also met, on one memorable occasion, Mick Jagger. As Vera recalls the meeting, she keeps her voice low
so that Dee Dee, who is now in the bedroom with the door
open, will not overhear. "He tried to pick me up right in
front of *him* [she nods in Dee Dee's direction] at a party in
Beverly Hills. And he was being so obvious about it that
it was getting downright embarrassing. He was really drunk,
and it was Thanksgiving, and a bunch of us (Jackson
Browne included) were sitting there, and he wouldn't stop.
Mick was asking me to sit on his lap. He had his arm around
me, holding my hand. Dee Dee was in shock. He wouldn't
speak up. And finally the best man who was at our wed-

ding, he knew Mick and he told him, 'You know, Mick, she's married.' And he was then married to Bianca. He goes, 'So, aren't we all?' Typical attitude. I imagine Jerry has her problems with him."

These days, Vera and Dee Dee are, at long last, stable. "We've gotten to the point where we're planning our lives ahead," says Vera. "We're making plans to have a family and move out of the apartment and get a house. It's really nice to know that you're going to stay with that particular person," she says with a smile. "We love each other more now than we did six years ago, because then it was just like, 'Wow, we're in love, and he's in a rock group, and we're touring all over the world.' "

Recently Vera, who had stopped working to help Dee Dee through his troubles, went back to work—this time in real estate. "It's the first time I've been back to work and not having to baby-sit. I didn't have any worries about 'Well, I'm going to go to work and I wonder what he's going to do.' I've gotten over that. Now I'm working again I feel like I'm doing something productive and something real."

Dee Dee, who has wandered back to the living room, a cup of coffee in hand, says he thinks that they will make more money from the real estate work than from his music. "The music is almost like a hobby," he says.

If that is the case now, can Dee Dee see himself being a Ramone when he's forty? "Sure," he answers. "The Ramones could keep going for a long time. We don't need a hit record to sell out shows. We're a legend."

Vera breaks in: "What else are you going to do when you've been a rock star for fifteen years—go work in Roy Rogers'?"

Dee Dee chuckles. "I'll have to go work in the supermarket. I'd be packing those bags. Or I'm going to play my piano in the park for pennies and quarters and give little concerts. Maybe with an accordion and a monkey. Easy work."

David Wolff

CYNDI LAUPER

"We gave each other the tools to succeed. And we gave each other a lot of love."

*N*ow that we've seen what life is like for women with rock stars, let's turn the tables and take a look at what it's like to be the male companion of a female rock star. David Wolff, thirty-five, is both boyfriend and manager to Cyndi Lauper, who, with hits like "Girls Just Want to Have Fun," "She-Bop," and "Time After Time," a carrot-colored razor-cut hairdo, mismatched clothes, and tons of clunky jewelry, has turned out to be one of the biggest singing and video sensations of the eighties.

While some men may very well find it difficult to be in the shadow of a famous female pop star, Dave Wolff says he has no problems with it at all. This probably has a lot to do with the stages that David and Cyndi were at in their careers when they met on Pearl Harbor Day in 1981. At that time, Cyndi's career as a singer was pretty much going nowhere. She had just left her group, Blue Angel, she was bankrupt, and she had no manager. David, on the other hand, had just started his own rock artist management company after many futile years spent trying to become a rock star himself. He felt very secure with his decision to leave the performing side of the music business. "When I was a musician, I was a frustrated manager," he says. "So it's not like as a manager I'm a frustrated musician."

Soon after he and Cyndi started going out, Cyndi played Dave an album she had cut with Blue Angel. "I acknowledged that she had a really good voice, but I didn't really know that she was as talented as she is," Dave recalls. "Then two or three weeks later she had a gig at the Ritz and she really freaked me out." He and Cyndi talked about having a working relationship, but Cyndi in the beginning was against it. "She was afraid that if we worked together, because of the pressures of the business, which are really amazing, that that would destroy our relationship. So she felt that she wanted to keep it apart, and then she was considering going with one particular manager and she was having nightmares about it. It was at that point that we decided, 'Why don't we do this together?' " And that's how the partnership began.

■ ■ ■

David Wolff leans back on a couch in the East Side Manhattan apartment that he shares with Cyndi Lauper and takes a sip of beer. He looks as relaxed as anyone could hope to look who has only a few days to attend to several weeks' worth of phone messages and laundry and a million other things before he can join Cyndi on the road in Florida. As for the apartment, well, judging from the decor, one gets the impression that neither Dave nor Cyndi spends much time there. Aside from the few little kitschy touches—pink flamingo statues and a pillow with a picture of the Washington Monument—the place is really quite bare. There are no pictures on the wall, and in one corner a box serves as a makeshift table.

And the truth is, says Dave, since Cyndi's meteoric rise to fame, they haven't been at home much. "We have not stopped working since we started this," says Dave. "We took four days in Bermuda, and that was it. It took us three days to wind down, and when we finally wound down, it was time to leave, and then everyone on the island knew we were there." Dave shakes his head and takes another swallow of beer. His looks—intense, almost Manson-like blue eyes framed by nearly shoulder-length brown hair and a beard—and his clothes—jeans, yellow shirt worn over a black T-shirt, and sneakers—are unexpected. Somehow you wouldn't think that someone like Cyndi, with her dis-

tinctly wacky eighties looks, would end up with a guy who
looks like a hippie. Apparently neither did Cyndi, at first.
In addition to the long hair and beard, when she met him,
Dave was wearing bellbottoms. "Cyndi didn't like me at
all!" says Dave. "She thought, 'Oh, God, this guy is right
out of the seventies!' But as it were, it didn't matter in the
end."

David's interest in the music business goes back to 1964,
when he was fifteen. The Beatles had just taken the world
by storm and, like many teen-age boys at that time, Dave
fantasized about becoming a rock and roll star. He joined
a band in his hometown of Stamford, Connecticut, called
the Chanters. At seventeen, he played guitar for a band
called the Corporate Image. "That band had a full-page
spread in *Seventeen* magazine in January 1967," he remembers. "I thought I was going to be a star." No such luck,
although he kept on chasing after fame with a number of
different bands for the next fifteen years. He played in
bands on weekends while he was a business major at Bab-
son College in Wellesley, Massachusetts—the decision to
go on to college having been made after David assessed his
musical abilities. "I wasn't very good, but I got by—barely,"
says Dave. "I wanted to get a business degree just so I'd
have something to fall back on in anticipation of not making it as a singer, knowing deep down inside that I wasn't
very good. No one had to tell me that. I always knew I
was going to end up in business, but I decided to take a
route so that I could do the things I wanted to do, knowing that at some point I really had to get down to it. So I
just delayed the inevitable as long as I could."

For someone who gives himself such a low rating in terms
of his performing abilities, David managed to get quite a
few breaks along the way. In 1976 he got his first record
deal with Phantom Records (which was distributed by RCA)
doing a novelty song about the Bicentennial called "Happy
Birthday USA" under the name of Kid Cashmere. "I sang

it with this other kid, Vinnie Vincent, who was the last guitar player for Kiss. It wasn't very good but it was funny. We dubbed in an audience, but we put so much of it in there, it sounded like static electricity throughout the whole song. It sold fifty records." Then, in 1978, he cut an album for Buddah Records, this time under his own name. "I sang *that* one in falsetto, not in my real voice, 'cause I couldn't sing. At least when I sang in falsetto, I could keep in pitch."

In performance, he wore a bow tie that flashed, a checkered suit, one white shoe, one black shoe, and a cape. The second record sold 200 copies and played on "maybe five stations," says Dave. "After that, it looked like the Kid was washed up." But then, somehow, another record deal came through. This time Dave rapped his way through a song called "Grab Them Cakes" under the name Captain Chameleon. "It got a lot of plays in discos, but it didn't catch on."

To support himself through lean times, Dave had a series of odd jobs—everything from delivering newspapers to being an exterminator. "When I went to apply for that exterminating job, I wore a short-hair wig. My real hair was halfway down my back, and I knew I needed a straight job and I didn't want to cut my hair, so I put it all in a wig. Plus I gave him a picture of some chick I was going out with and I said, 'This is my fiancée,' because they want to hire married people. They hired me. But the next day I showed up for work and I had my hair in a ponytail, and the guy looked at me like, 'Oh, man. You didn't look like that yesterday. You better be real good at this.' They watched me like a hawk. But after a month, I quit. I hated it."

After "Grab Them Cakes" stiffed, a lawyer friend of David's took him aside and said, "Why don't you apply all the skills that you are natural at toward other people and start a management company?" "It had been something over the last four or five years every now and then he'd throw at me," says Dave. "My strengths lie in putting packages together and organizing packages. But being the object of all that organization was where it normally fell down. So I said, 'Okay, I'll do it.' " So, in January 1981 David opened up a management company, 65 West Entertainment, in Manhattan. By December it looked like his business was starting to get off the ground. He had signed up several artists, including a group called the Major Thinkers.

David Wolff and Cyndi Lauper.

By contrast, his love life was foundering. "I was seeing this other girl who was seeing somebody else at the time. I was supposed to see her one night, and she called me up and said, 'I can't go. I have this other problem.' I was really pissed." So Dave was on his way home to Connecticut that night when, on the spur of the moment, he decided to stop by at a surprise birthday party in New York for a friend who was the bass player in Blue Angel, Cyndi's group. "I

stopped in, and Cyndi was there. She was blond then. I
didn't know who she was. I started talking to this other
girl at the party and I tried to pick her up and I was doing
okay until she told me she had a boyfriend. She got up to
go to the bathroom, and when she got up to go, I sat down
with Cyndi. And Cyndi had been listening to all the bullshit
I was handing out to her. She didn't like this at all. At first
she was giving me a lot of shit, but I was very persistent.
I told Cyndi all about rock pygmies and all these guys in
ancient Babylonian culture, and she really got into that. I
just remember having a great time, once she got over what
she had just watched me doing. We ended up leaving the
party together. I gave her a ride home, and we've been together ever since, from that night on."

For Dave, Cyndi was and still is very different from the
girls he'd gone out with in the past. "She's very sincere,
very genuine. She knows what she wants. She's got an incredible amount of talent, a lot of love, and she's a dynamite person. She gives me more love than anybody else
ever did—that's real. And I give it back. And I never had
that before. We gave each other fulfillment emotionally."

In 1981 Cyndi's career wasn't going very well. "She was
getting nowhere, as talented as she was," says Dave. So,
six months into the relationship, they overcame their hes-
itations and became a working team. Says Dave, "She
needed somebody who really cared and had the ability to
take her up. A lot of people tried and failed, and look how
great she is. And for me in business, I needed something
that great to use my talents. We gave each other the tools
to succeed. And we gave each other a lot of love."

Before they could get down to the business of music,
however, there were quite a few things in Cyndi's life that
needed clearing up. "All she had was lawsuits. She had no
current songs, no band, no money. We got a bankruptcy
lawyer who did an incredible job of protecting her from
her former manager, who was suing her for a lot of money—

unjustifiably. And we organized the case together, and I did a lot of research, and so did he, and we put together a package and we won. We got all her songs back, only had to pay a little bit of money. There was nobody who could harm her. At that point, when we cleaned up her whole past, then we started taking care of the creative thing." And it was on the creative end that David feels he was different from Cyndi's other managers.

"I think Cyndi's talent and her instincts are so right on that not to go with that would be ineffective management and management running scared," he says. "All the other people she'd hooked up with in the past didn't know how to channel her talent to help her succeed as she was. They only wanted to change her, whether it was to change her looks, her image, her music. So I didn't threaten her in terms of changing her. I just let her be whatever she wanted. That's what I would promote: who she was. We got her a producer, Rick Chertoff; got her songs. She started writing and got new songwriters. Then we got the whole album done, got a band, made a video, we made posters, we made pictures. The whole CBS company was educated as to who this lady was." (Even before he was officially managing Cyndi, David managed to talk an old friend from his band-playing days who was now head of CBS Portrait Records into flying down to Puerto Rico to see Cyndi perform. Cyndi was signed to CBS shortly thereafter.)

The transition from promoting himself as a performer to promoting Cyndi was surprisingly easy for David. "In my life this has been the one project in terms of business that I really believed was going to succeed. All the other projects I worked on, I hoped I would have success. This one— if there's any way to know it, I knew it. Before it all happened, when nothing was going on, everybody I spoke to I said, 'This lady is going to be the biggest female attraction in the world.' And I always risked people saying, 'What an asshole.' "

For the first year of their partnership, Cyndi and David didn't let anyone know that they were romantically involved. "We didn't want *that* to interfere with our progress in the business. We knew what we were doing in business, but a lot of times people are critical, and they look for anything to make an excuse to stop you from succeeding, and sometimes they misjudge or look down on that kind of relationship in this business. So we didn't give anybody any ammunition. We always registered in two rooms on the road. Which we still do, because she's got her trunks and everything. We just carried on very professionally—we never held hands or any of that stuff. It was always business, and she'd always refer to me as her manager. And I would refer to her as my artist. We just did the best we could, set everything right, and then we started to succeed, and I was in her 'Time After Time' video. Then we just decided, 'Well, it doesn't matter anymore. We're getting over as a team.'"

Would the team have been as successful if, say, they hadn't had a personal relationship as well? David answers, "I would have given her as much attention, but I don't believe that it would have worked this way. I think that the fact that we did this together on so many levels made it a little bit easier to deal with everything that had to be done to create this. I had all day, every day, to think about it and work it out. Whereas if I were her manager on the outside, there would be all that time that we wouldn't be together to create doubt and confusion."

A good portion of whatever free time Cyndi and Dave have together is spent discussing business. "But we still have our time together as well. When we come home, we still hang out, watch *The Honeymooners*, play cards. Sort of freak out, talk to each other, like 'Do you believe this?' "

While Dave insists that fame hasn't affected their personal relationship, he admits that it has affected their lifestyle. "What's changed is that I have to do the shopping because she can't. She'll get mobbed. We're moving. We bought a condominium in SoHo. When we first started living together, we were living on the fifth floor of a five-floor walk-up. One room. Loftbed. That was a drag. And the guy across the hall smelled. That was rough. And I had a car. And every morning at eight o'clock I had to change the parking because I couldn't afford a parking lot. This was only a year ago. And now, everybody calls. I get a hundred calls a day from nine-thirty in the morning to seven-thirty at night. The phone never stops.

"We're making money, but it still hasn't sunk in yet, the fact that we can afford things. We're so used to not having it that we're just trying to get used to this. And then you've got to be careful when you get used to this because you don't know if it's going to last or to what extent. Suppose you have a bad year, and you have all these things that you want to buy and maintain. You've got to be really smart when you first arrive on the block."

One thing that they're not investing their money in is hard drugs. Says David, "I've never done cocaine in my life. I don't even like nasal spray. Cyndi's straight too, and she's very concerned about her voice and her exercises to keep her voice in shape."

When asked if he and Cyndi plan to get married, Dave looks surprised. "We don't have any plans to get married," he answers. "This is pretty cool the way it is." As for kids, they really haven't thought about it, he says. "It's kind of hard to sit down and reflect what's really going on, *what* you can really plan together."

Cyndi, as everybody knows, is an avowed feminist. Dave, on the other hand, is a little shy about actively aligning himself with any cause. "I don't like all the marching—for any cause. But I'm not a chauvinist—I do understand the feminist point of view. I don't hurt her, I don't treat her bad. I don't abuse anybody!"

All of a sudden David stops talking and cocks an ear toward the open window. Out on the street below, there is a major traffic jam, and as usual, impatient New York cabbies are taking out their frustrations on their horns. But somewhere above the cacophony, one can hear, very faintly, the sound of a radio playing. "Listen," Dave says looking very pleased. "It's Cyndi's song. 'All Through the Night.' If it gets into the Top Ten, she'll be the first artist in the history of our industry to have four Top Tens on a debut album." And sure enough, not long after the interview, it made it into the Top Ten.

Victoria Balfour has written for
The New York Times, *Esquire*, and *USA Today*.
Rock Wives is her first book.